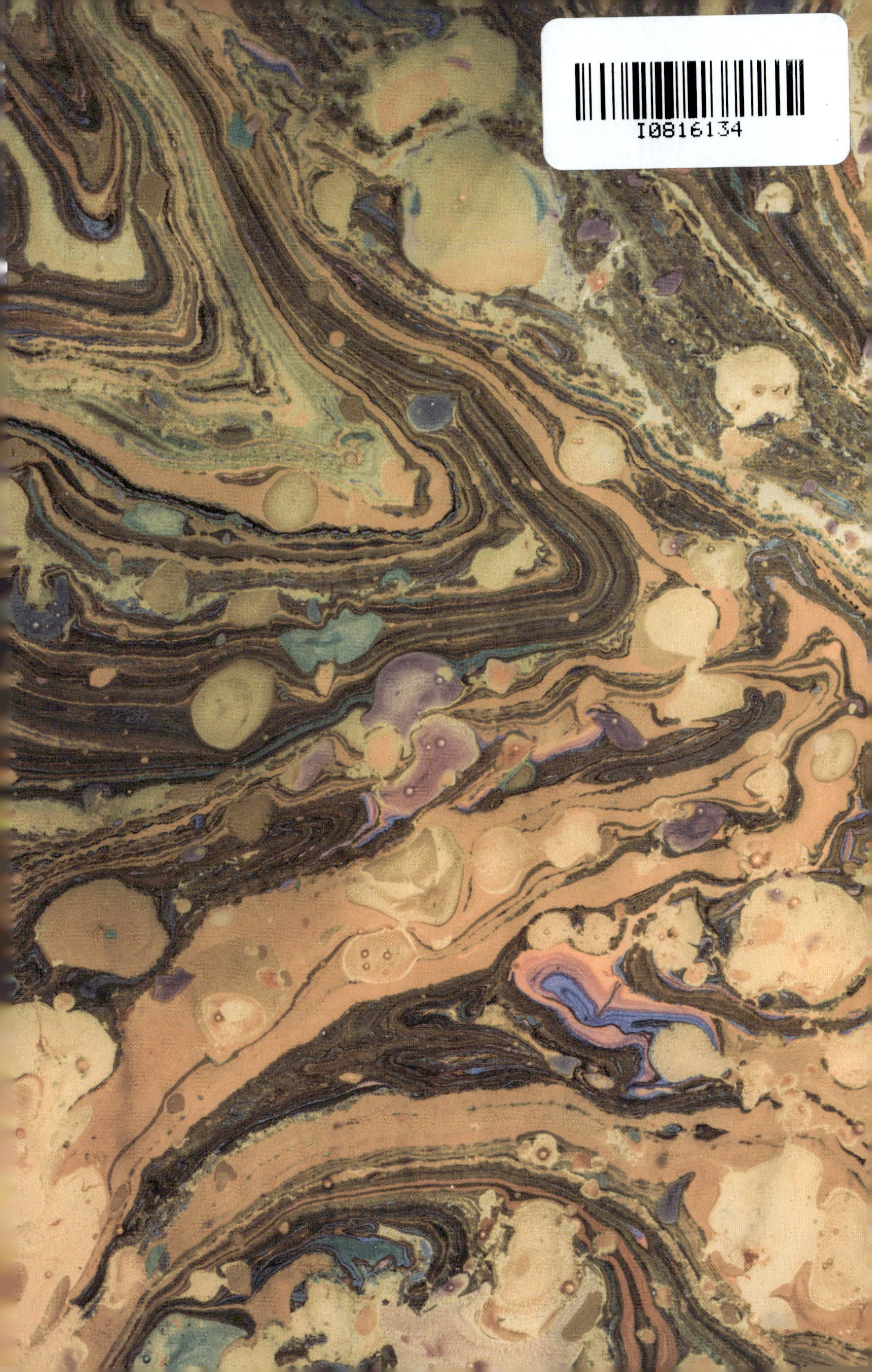
I0816134

THE DOCTRINES *of* GRACE

THE DOCTRINES *of* GRACE

DESIGNED BY WEKREATIVE CO.
ISBN: 978-1-883973-20-9
PRINTED IN CHINA

MacArthur
PREACHING CLASSICS

Over five decades of faithful, verse-by-verse exposition, John MacArthur has produced a vast collection of Bible teaching. For new readers and listeners, the quantity alone can be intimidating. With a library of more than 3,500 sermons, where do you begin?

MacArthur Preaching Classics presents some of John's best and most beloved sermons, edited for print while maintaining their personal and practical qualities. These collections are packed with powerful, life-transforming truth you'll want to share with others and revisit to refresh your own soul.

This first volume, based on *The Doctrines of Grace* sermon series, is a prime example of how John MacArthur's expository preaching makes the hard truths of Scripture simple, and the complex clear. It centers on giving God all the glory for His saving work, and puts the focus where John always puts it—on the non-negotiable authority and clarity of God's Word.

CONTENTS

ABSOLUTE INABILITY

"WE ARE SO ENTIRELY CONTROLLED BY THE POWER OF SIN, THAT THE WHOLE MIND, THE WHOLE HEART, AND ALL OUR ACTIONS ARE UNDER ITS INFLUENCE."

JOHN CALVIN[1]

UNWILLING AND UNABLE

Through all my years of preaching, I have predominantly worked verse by verse through texts of Scripture. So when I leave that flow of exposition and embark on a topical or doctrinal study, I potentially open myself to the accusation that I may be caught up in something philosophical or drawing from an authority other than Scripture. But I don't want to present you conclusions built on my own speculation—I want to bring you what the very Word of God has to say on this important doctrinal issue. I would encourage you, like the noble Bereans, to do a little work yourself and search the Bible to see if these things are so (Acts 17:11).

This book concerns the sovereignty of God in salvation. But any discussion on that topic must begin with another doctrine: what I'm going to call *absolute inability*. God must be sovereign in our salvation precisely because we are neither willing nor able to choose salvation for ourselves.

TOTALLY DEPRAVED?

The doctrine of absolute inability is commonly called "total depravity," but I think that is a misleading term. If you look up *depravity* in the dictionary, it's a synonym for *viciousness*. In fact, to be depraved is to be degraded and immoral to a dangerous degree, like a serial killer. The word *depraved* can connote a level of evil that's not applicable to everybody. And to say a person is *totally* depraved seemingly puts them on par with someone like Jeffrey Dahmer or Charles Manson. That is not what theologians mean when they speak of total depravity.

Not everybody is as bad as they could be, and not everybody is as bad as everybody else. What we're talking about in this doctrine is our inability to respond to the gospel correctly or do any spiritual good whatsoever. We are completely unable to raise ourselves out of a state of spiritual death. We lack the ability to give sight to our blind hearts. We are entirely incapable of freeing ourselves from slavery to sin. We cannot turn ourselves from ignorance to truth. We are utterly powerless to stop rebelling against God and His Word.

For this reason, I prefer to use the term *absolute inability* instead of *total depravity*.

THE MOST HATED CHRISTIAN DOCTRINE

Speaking in the upper room, Jesus warned His disciples about the opposition they—and all His followers throughout church history—were bound to face. "If the world hates you, you know that it has hated Me before it hated you" (John 15:18).

Why did the world hate Christ? How could they despise the most marvelous, compassionate, gentle, merciful, gracious, kind, and loving human who ever walked the earth? How could they loathe the God-Man who expressed divine love through abject humility, and ultimately death, as a sacrifice for sin? How could they hate the one who provided an entrance into His heavenly kingdom and eternal life? Realistically, it would have been difficult to hate Jesus. He banished illness from the land of Israel for three years. He cared for children and widows and all kinds of suffering people. He brought a message of forgiveness, salvation, joy, and peace. He gave hope to the hopeless, offering freedom from the bondage of sin, and the hope of heaven. *And they hated Him*. Why?

Earlier in John's gospel, Jesus explained, "The world ... hates Me because I testify of it, that its deeds are evil" (7:7).

Fallen man does not want to be confronted with the true nature of his heart. He doesn't want to face his inherent wickedness. He has to find a way to tolerate and excuse himself from the guilt he naturally faces each day. So he falls back on his most dominant sin, pride, and imagines a version of himself that can escape condemnation. He spins a web of delusions, convincing himself that he is truly good and noble—anything to distract from the fact that his deeds are evil.

The Jewish leaders hated Christ because He cut through their self-deception and exposed the wickedness of their hearts and the corruption of their religion. And as you go through John's gospel, you see their hate expressed throughout the whole record of our Lord's life. John 5:16 says, "The Jews were persecuting Jesus, because He was doing these things on the Sabbath." They hated Him for exposing the emptiness of their religion of works. Verse 18 adds, "The Jews were seeking all the more to kill Him"—it's only John 5, and they already want Him dead. This early into His public ministry, they were already plotting His murder "because He not only was breaking the Sabbath, but also was calling God His own Father, making Himself equal with God." In John 7:32 the officers of the Pharisees were sent to seize Him. In John 8 and again in chapter 10, they picked up rocks to stone Him to death. In John 11 they plotted to kill Him—and eventually they succeeded, arresting, beating, scourging, and ultimately crucifying Him. From the beginning to the end of His public ministry, He was met with constant hostility.

And throughout those three years, He was always clear about the depth of their sinfulness. John 8 recounts a confrontation between Jesus and a group of Jewish leaders attempting to defend their ethnic and religious credentials. In verse 41, they asserted, "We have one Father: God." The Lord replied, "If God were your Father, you would love Me, for I proceeded forth and have come from God, for I have not even come on My own initiative, but He sent Me" (v. 42). It's really that simple—you can't claim to love the Father if you hate His Son.

In verse 43, He began to diagnose the source of their disdain. "Why do you not understand what I am saying? It is because you cannot hear My word." He was identifying how deep and all-encompassing their sin was. He was showing them the futility and emptiness of their religiosity—they were so corrupt that they couldn't even understand what He was saying. Why?

"You are of your father the devil" (v. 44). Talk about offensive. He told these Jewish leaders to their faces that they were operating under the power of Satan. This was an overt assault on the spiritual superiority that they lorded over all of Israel. They represented the pinnacle of piety, but Christ was exposing them for frauds. "You are of your father the devil, and you want to do the desires of your father. He was a murderer from the beginning"—He knew the intention of their hearts was to kill Him, and He exposed their wicked motives to everyone within earshot.

But it wasn't just their murderous desires that identified them as sons of Satan. Jesus continued, "He was a murderer from the beginning, and does not stand in the truth because there is no truth in him. Whenever he speaks a lie, he speaks from his own nature, for he is a liar and the father of lies" (v. 44). This is a profound diagnosis of the human condition: "You cannot understand the Word of God. You do not love the Father or His Son. Instead, you follow *your* father, the devil, and you do what he desires to do—namely, to murder and spread his lies."

Jesus makes an amazing statement in verse 45, "But because I speak the truth, you do not believe Me." We need to consider that in the context of evangelism. When you give someone the gospel, they do not have in themselves the capacity to believe it, because it is the truth. *Because* it's God's truth, they cannot receive it. They are predisposed to believe lies. In verse 47, Jesus adds, "He who is of God hears the words of God; for this reason you do not hear them, because you are not of God." Essentially He's saying, "If you belonged to God, you would love His Word. But you belong to Satan, and you follow his desires and live under his control, so you have no capacity to believe the truth. And because I speak the truth, you don't believe Me—and you hate Me."

All of that was intensely offensive to the Jewish religious leaders. They prided themselves as the experts on God and His Word. They conducted themselves as His representatives. But Christ was peeling away their pious façade. In an attempt to claw back some of their lost credibility, they accused Him of having a demon (v. 48). That's how upside-down the sinner's worldview is—he is so dominated by demonic lies that he lacks the capacity to recognize God and His truth. It's such a profane inversion that he will accuse the Son of God of being demon possessed.

Christ continued to confront their sinful unbelief. "I do not have a demon; but I honor My Father, and you dishonor Me" (v. 49). He said, "Truly, truly, I say to you, if anyone keeps My word he will never see death" (v. 51). Their only response was to persist in their spiritual blindness: "Now we know that You have a demon" (v. 52). He was offering them eternal life, and they said, "You're from hell."

There is no evangelistic strategy that can overcome that kind of staunch unbelief and sinful resistance. There's no spin you can put on the truth of sin and its comprehensive corruption that can make it acceptable and attractive to the sinner. Unrepentant humans don't want to deal with the truth of the human condition—that they are lost, blind, ignorant, and dead. They're stuck in the slavery of sin and under the control of satanic power. They cannot accept that truth, no matter how winsomely you speak it.

It doesn't matter how glorious the offer of heaven and eternal life is to the sinner, because it's predicated on the recognition that they are children of Satan and profoundly captive to sin. Their corrupt, rebellious hearts simply won't tolerate that truth.

The doctrine of absolute inability is the most hated Christian doctrine because it makes clear the profound depths of the sinner's corruption—so corrupt that the truth sounds like a demonic lie. The natural man is utterly incapable of recognizing or believing biblical truth. And he hates facing those facts.

Consequently, this is also the most *minimized* Christian doctrine. For many believers, there is a natural tendency to avoid talking about the true condition of the nonbeliever because it is so intensely offensive. Some see it as a barrier they need to overcome through cleverness and ingenuity. The entire seeker-sensitive movement sprang forth from the desire to make the harsh truths of the gospel less offensive and more engaging.

The sinner's absolute inability *is* a barrier—but it's a truth we must embrace. In His wisdom, God has woven into the gospel the offensive truth about the sinner's corrupt condition as an obstacle to superficial acceptance. A gospel that doesn't assault the nonbeliever's pride—one that coddles his self-delusion rather than confronting him with the reality of his sin and the judgment that demands—is no gospel at all. The good news of the gospel is only good news if the bad news about the human condition is first understood.

The true gospel of Jesus Christ will offend. It will generate hatred and hostility from the world—sinners are trapped in such pervasive darkness that they cannot respond otherwise. God's people need the courage of conviction to bring such unpopular truth to men and women who desperately need it, regardless of the opposition we will endure.

THE MOST DISTINCTIVELY CHRISTIAN DOCTRINE

The world's fierce opposition to the doctrine of absolute inability is the reason this doctrine is unique to biblical Christianity. No other religion includes it, or anything remotely like it, because they all rely on good works for salvation.

All religions, including all the false forms of Christianity, affirm that people are inherently good, or at least still have some good in them—a kind of prevenient grace that allows them to contribute to their own salvation. They can choose to believe. They can choose to be saved. They can bring something to the table—through their religiosity, their morality, or their innate goodness—and make a contribution to their own salvation. Every false religion vigorously promotes this lie.

You can understand why works righteousness is a hallmark of man-made religion. It's the lie that blunts the sharp edges of the gospel, preserving man's pride while assuaging his guilt. Religion tells him that he's not so bad after all—that he's part of the solution rather than all of the problem.

Only biblical Christianity says that the sinner brings nothing. "For by grace you have been saved through faith; and that *not of yourselves*, it is the gift of God; *not as a result of works, so that no one may boast*" (Eph 2:8–9, emphasis added). Grace isn't grace if you have to add human works to it.

It's worth noting that religion is never a step toward God. Over the years, ecumenism has steadily crept into the church, assaulting the exclusivity of Christ. Today, many professing believers are convinced that God accepts the worship of all religions, including Judaism and even Islam.[2] But those false religions are never a step toward God. In fact, they are the final blasphemy.

Man is never more sinful than when he is inventing a false god or a false Christ. It is the epitome of wicked depravity for the sinner to create a god whose standard of goodness is low enough for the sinner's own corrupt works to save him. Scripture is clear that the sinner's best works are still entirely worthless. Isaiah 64:6 identifies man's attempts at righteousness as nothing more than "filthy rags" (NKJV). There is no step toward God through man-made religion. The false religions of the world are in an all-out sprint *away* from the truth of the gospel. They're an attempt to soothe the sinner's conscience while undermining the only truth that offers hope of salvation and redemption.

This is the challenge for the true church when it comes to the work of the gospel. The good news of Jesus Christ must begin with confronting the sinner's need for a Savior. There is no good news if we don't first establish the bad news. God's people must be up front with the truth of the sinner's absolute inability, confronting the lies of false religion on the very doctrinal ground they exist to obscure.

DEATH AS AN ANALOGY

Having considered those distinctions, it's time we delve into the doctrine itself. God's Word provides us with a helpful analogy to understand the depth of absolute inability. While the analogy is used throughout Scripture, we find it most vividly deployed in John 11. This memorable chapter records the resurrection of one of Jesus' most intimate friends, a man named Lazarus. Lazarus had two sisters named Mary and Martha, who were also close friends of Jesus.

The chapter opens with the news that Lazarus became ill (John 11:2). His sisters sent a message to Jesus saying, "Lord, behold, he whom You love is sick" (v. 3). That Lazarus is called "he whom You love" indicates that Jesus had a special affection for Lazarus. Hearing that His friend had fallen ill, Jesus says in verse 4, "This sickness is not to end in death, but for the glory of God, so that the Son of God may be glorified by it." God had a purpose in the sickness, and it was far bigger than the death of Lazarus. Verse 5 reemphasizes the fact that Jesus loved Lazarus and his two sisters. But even upon receiving the news, Jesus stayed two days longer in the place where He was, without responding (v. 6).

When Jesus finally arrived, He was late by Mary and Martha's standards. Verse 17 says, "He found that [Lazarus] had already been in the tomb four days." Verse 19 paints the dreary picture that Jesus walked into: "And many of the Jews had come to Martha and Mary, to console them concerning their brother." This was a kind of community activity that happened when there was a death. Everybody surrounded the mourning family to grieve along with them as a form of comfort.

As Jesus arrived, Martha approached Him in grief, saying, "Lord, if You had been here, my brother would not have died" (v. 21). She had great confidence in Jesus (v. 22), but apparently that confidence did not extend to His power to resurrect.

Verses 23–27 record the rest of their theologically dense conversation.

> Jesus said to her, "Your brother will rise again." Martha said to Him, "I know that he will rise again in the resurrection on the last day." Jesus said to her, "I am the resurrection and the life; he who believes in Me will live even if he dies, and everyone who lives and believes in Me will never die. Do you believe this?" She said to Him, "Yes, Lord; I have believed that You are the Christ, the Son of God, even He who comes into the world."

Martha looked forward to the final resurrection as the only hope for her brother. And as the story goes on, Mary comes to Jesus with the same lament, "Lord if You had been here, my brother would not have died" (v. 32).

At this point, when He saw the weeping sisters and the mourning crowd, Jesus was deeply moved (v. 33). The story continues,

> [Jesus] said, "Where have you laid him?" They said to Him, "Lord, come and see." Jesus wept. So the Jews were saying, "See how He loved him!" But some of them said, "Could not this man, who opened the eyes of the blind man, have kept this man also from dying?"
>
> So Jesus, again being deeply moved within, came to the tomb. Now it was a cave, and a stone was lying against it. Jesus said, "Remove the stone." Martha, the sister of the deceased, said to Him, "Lord, by this time there will be a stench, for he has been

> dead four days." Jesus said to her, "Did I not say to you that if you believe, you will see the glory of God?" So they removed the stone. Then Jesus raised His eyes, and said, "Father, I thank You that You have heard Me. I knew that You always hear Me; but because of the people standing around I said it, so that they may believe that You sent Me." (vv. 34–42)

Finally, verse 43 records, "When He had said these things, He cried out with a loud voice, 'Lazarus, come forth.'"

What is interesting here is that Jesus gave a command *to a dead man*. I've done a lot of funerals and seen a lot of dead people, but I've never asked any of them to do anything. I would certainly never say to a dead man, "Come forth!" I'd look foolish.

Dead men can't hear. They can't think. They can't respond. Dead men are absolutely unable to react to any kind of stimulus. They lack any power to act. But amazingly, verse 44 says, "The man who had died came forth."

Lazarus did exactly what Jesus directed him to do. As I've just said, dead men can't obey commands—but Lazarus did. He did the impossible. How? Because Christ gave him the ability to obey.

If Christ hadn't given him life, Lazarus couldn't have responded. That's what is bound up in Jesus' earlier words, in verses 25 and 26: "I am the resurrection and the life." This amazing miracle of giving a dead man the power to respond is analogous to salvation. The gospel commands dead men to understand, believe, and repent. Frankly, the gospel commands dead people to do what they are unable to do.

DEAD IN SIN

In spiritual terms, we were all once like Lazarus. If you have not yet believed in the substitutionary death of Christ and repented of your sins, you *still are* just like Lazarus: dead and unable to respond. In Ephesians 2:1, Paul bluntly describes the spiritual condition of every sinner, "You were dead in your trespasses and sins."

We were all dead. Man's basic problem is not a lack of self-esteem. It's not an issue of his environment. It's not that he needs to make a few minor adjustments to get God on his side. Man's problem is that he is absolutely dead and, therefore, incapable of responding to God's truth or commands. What were we dead to? We were dead to God, to spiritual reality, and to the truth.

We know this is the case because "the wages of sin is death" (Rom 6:23). Sin kills. The Bible frequently reiterates that we were not only spiritually ignorant, blind, or weak—we were *completely dead*.

In Matthew's gospel, after Jesus invites a man to become one of His disciples, that man replied, "Lord, permit me first to go and bury my father" (Matt 8:21). In the next verse Jesus responded, "Follow Me, and allow the dead to bury their own dead." He was saying, "Let the spiritually dead bury the physically dead." Jesus refers to those outside His kingdom as "dead."

In 1 Timothy 5:6, Paul says, "She who gives herself to wanton pleasure is dead even while she lives." Here again, Scripture speaks of unbelievers as *dead*. Not merely sick or weak, but completely dead and unable to respond to God.

Back in Paul's letter to the Ephesians, the apostle describes unbelievers with these words: "The Gentiles also walk, in the futility of their mind, being darkened in their understanding, excluded from the life of God" (Eph 4:17–18). This is another way of saying "dead in sin." To be "excluded from the life of God" is to be spiritually dead. Unbelievers are physically alive but spiritually dead.

Colossians 2:13 weighs in on this as well. Paul writes, "When you were dead in your transgressions and the uncircumcision of your flesh, He made you alive." In the Greek, the phrase "dead in your transgressions" refers to a sphere or a realm. Unbelievers live in the realm of death. In this realm, like people who are physically dead, unbelievers are devoid of any spiritual sense, dominated entirely by their sinful desires. And it is while people are still lost in that spiritually dead condition that God makes them alive.

This is the same image Paul paints back in Ephesians 2:1. In verse 2, he adds that unbelievers live "according to the course of this world." The Greek term for "world" here is *kosmos*, and it doesn't refer to the physical world. It has to do with the sinful system of humanity and Satan. That's why Jesus called Satan "the ruler of this world" (John 12:31). In other words, the sinner lives according to the sinful world's standards and values. He is conducting himself in complete harmony with the spirit of the age. This is the doctrine of absolute inability—it means you're locked into a cycle of sin that you can't escape, walking in the spirit of the age.

Not only do unbelievers live according to the sinful system of the world, but Paul goes on in Ephesians 2:2 to state that they live "according to the prince of the power of the air." This doesn't mean that everybody is literally indwelt by Satan, like Judas was. Rather, it means that Satan is behind the influences and trends of the world. Paul even calls him "the god of this age" (2 Cor 4:4, NKJV).

So mankind lives according to the course of this sinful world, under the influence and will of Satan, and lastly, Paul adds in verse 3 of Ephesians 2, "Among them we too all formerly lived in the lusts of our flesh, indulging the desires of the flesh and of the mind, and were by nature children of wrath, even as the rest." "Flesh" in this verse refers to man's fallen nature (cf. Gal 5:16). So all humanity is driven by the lusts and desires of their sinful nature. And because of this inability to do anything but fulfill their own sinful desires, everyone is a child of wrath. In other words, they are the targets for God's judgment.

The sinner is so dead in sin that his whole life is summed up as being controlled by the world, the devil, and the flesh. He can do absolutely nothing outside of those influences. Just like Lazarus in the tomb, the unregenerate sinner is helpless to improve his spiritual condition by his own strength.

Even when salvation is introduced in Ephesians 2:4–5, Scripture doesn't say, "However, one day you came to your senses." It says, "But God, being rich in mercy, because of His great love with which He loved us, even when we were dead in our transgressions, made us alive." *God* made us alive. It is by His power *alone* that the spiritually dead come to life.

To be clear, I'm not saying that sinners can't do some human good. They can be philanthropic, kind, and merciful. But they cannot do any *spiritual* good. They cannot do anything that pleases God, because no one can do anything that pleases God unless it's done for His glory. So while there is human good, it is "dead" good. It has absolutely nothing to do with pleasing or honoring God.

In Luke 6:33, Jesus says, "If you do good to those who do good to you, what credit is that to you? For even sinners do the same." In human terms, sinners can treat each other with fairness and favor; they can show kindness and compassion. In Luke 11:13, He further acknowledges the kind of human good that sinners show to their children: "You then, being evil, know how to give good gifts to your children." So even Jesus admits that there is a sense in which unsaved people do good to each other. But it's merely a human good. There is nothing God-honoring about this good, nothing that merits blessing and favor from heaven's perspective. It is good in one sense, but bad in the sense that it has no pure motive. Nothing about it pleases God because it wasn't done to glorify Him (cf. Heb 11:6). It counts for absolutely nothing in terms of eternity.

A WHOLE RACE OF LAZARUSES

This condition of being spiritually dead is not the way humans were originally made by God. When God created Adam and Eve, they were spiritually alive. They communed with God. They walked and talked with Him in the cool of the day. They obeyed and loved God, and as you know, God gave them one prohibition: "From the tree of the knowledge of good and evil you shall not eat, for in the day that you eat from it you will surely die" (Gen 2:17).

But they did eat from the tree, and they did die spiritually. Genesis 3:1–6 records,

> Now the serpent was more crafty than any beast of the field which the Lord God had made. And he said to the woman, "Indeed, has God said, 'You shall not eat from any tree of the garden'?" The woman said to the serpent, "From the fruit of the trees of the garden we may eat; but from the fruit of the tree which is in the middle of the garden, God has said, 'You shall not eat from it or touch it, or you will die.'" The serpent said to the woman, "You surely will not die! For God knows that in the day you eat from it your eyes will be opened, and you will be like God, knowing good and evil." When the woman saw that the tree was good for food, and that it was a delight to the eyes, and that the tree was desirable to make *one* wise, she took from its fruit and ate; and she gave also to her husband with her, and he ate.

Immediately, Adam and Eve were alienated from God. They hid from Him (v. 7). And Adam's sin didn't lead to just his own spiritual death—it brought spiritual death to the whole human race. Even though Eve ate first, it was Adam's sin that corrupted mankind because he acted as the head of all humanity. That's Paul's point in Romans 5:12: "Through one man sin entered into the world, and death through sin, and so death spread to all men."

Sin exists because of the sin of one man. The whole complex of sin, death, and condemnation—all of it came through one man's act. The reign of sin over humanity is the result of Adam's disobedience. He was appointed the representative of man, and when he sinned, the whole human race was plunged into the slavery of sin and death. No one escapes.

Paul makes that clear in 1 Corinthians 15:22, putting it succinctly, "In Adam all die." We all demonstrate that we have Adam's corruption because we all die; and death is the penalty for sin. Even babies in the womb die before they ever had the opportunity to commit an act of sin (Rom 5:14). The corruption of Adam's sin and the reality of death abide in their very being.

Confessing his own sinfulness, David even says, "In sin my mother conceived me" (Ps 51:5). He doesn't mean he was an illegitimate child; he wasn't. He doesn't mean he was born out of some adulterous affair. What he means is that from conception, he was a sinner. Psalm 58:3 agrees: "The wicked are estranged from the womb." So Adam's act of defiance brought death into the world and caused us all to be born as sinners.

In the context of Romans 5:12, Paul is explaining to his readers how it was possible for the death of *one man*, Christ, to save *so many*. He explains it by showing that the sin of one man corrupted the whole human race: "Through one man sin entered into the world, and death through sin, and so death spread to all men." Adam acted as the representative head of the entire human race when he sinned in Eden.

The heretic Pelagius (AD 354–418) denied this reality by teaching that men are born innocent and become corrupted by their own sin instead of Adam's. But verse 18 refutes that heresy entirely: "So then as through one transgression there resulted condemnation to all men." It was "through *one* transgression" that humanity became a race of Lazaruses.[3]

Spurgeon explains this biblical truth: "Through the fall, and through our own sin, the nature of man has become so debased, so depraved, and corrupt, that it is impossible for him to come to Christ without the assistance of God the Holy Spirit.... [He] is so corrupt that he has neither the will nor the power to come to Christ unless drawn by the Spirit."[4]

People may hate the doctrine of absolute inability. They may resent the claim that they were born sinners. But their protests are useless in the face of the overwhelming proof—they all die. And their death proves that they, like the rest of mankind, were born dead in sin.

THE NEED FOR SPIRITUAL RESURRECTION

God originally made man upright, but now the whole of humanity is dead in trespasses and sins (cf. Eccl 7:29). God commands sinners to repent and believe (Mark 1:15). He commands them to believe in His Son, to love His Son, to confess His Son, and to submit to His Son. But you have to ask the question: How can a whole race of Lazaruses respond? How can a dead man choose to be alive?

This is the compelling question that lies behind the doctrine of election. If sinners are left to themselves to repent and believe, by what power do they do it? If you don't believe in divine election, or you believe that God bases election on knowledge of which people will choose to be saved, you must answer the question: *By what power* do they choose salvation? *By what power* does the dead man rise?

If God does not make sinners willing and able, where do the power and will come from? Those who deny election as a sovereign act of God have to believe that there's something in man that enables him to choose to come to life. But the Bible doesn't describe our condition as a disability or a handicap to overcome. It describes the sinner's spiritual state as *death*—and everyone knows that dead people are incapable of responding.

This is consistently taught throughout Scripture. John 1:12, for instance, says, "As many as received Him, to them He gave the right to become children of God, even to those who believe in His name." We love that verse; many people even memorize it. Yet we know that you can't be raised from the dead by your own choice. That's why verse 13 adds, "Who were born, not of blood nor of the will of the flesh nor of the will of man, but of God." Whoever received Christ, believed, and became a child of God was first *enabled by God*. It wasn't their own will that led them to believe; it was God.

In John chapter 3, probably one of the most familiar chapters in all the Bible, Jesus talks to Nicodemus about what it means to be born again. In verses 5 and 6, Jesus says, "Truly, truly, I say to you, unless one is born of water and the Spirit he cannot enter into the kingdom of God. That which is born of the flesh is flesh, and that which is born of the Spirit is spirit." He's referring there to regeneration—the work of the Holy Spirit described by Ezekiel in the great prophecy that talks about the New Covenant (Ezek 36:24–27).

You have to be born by the power of the Holy Spirit. You have to be cleansed from above. Then Jesus says this: "The wind blows where it wishes and you hear the sound of it, but do not know where it comes from and where it is going; so is everyone who is born of the Spirit" (John 3:8). What a statement! People can be born again only by the power of the Spirit, and He goes wherever He wants. *God's choice* is the determining factor in the new birth, not man's will.

Jesus makes the same point in John 5:21. "Just as the Father raises the dead and gives them life, even so the Son also gives life to whom He wishes." That is a painful verse to read if you deny the sovereignty of God in salvation. The Son gives life to whom He wishes, just as the Spirit gives life to whom He wishes (John 3). When somebody is raised to life, it's not by the will of man; it's by the will of God.

We see God's sovereign election not only in John 1, John 3, and John 5, but also in John 6. Verse 44 says, "No one can come to Me unless the Father who sent Me draws him." He repeats this idea in verse 65, "No one can come to Me unless it has been granted him from the Father." Unbelievers don't have a capacity to come to the Father. They are utterly unable to come to Christ because they are dead in sin. If they do come, it is only because the Father has given them the ability to come. This is why John Calvin wrote that unredeemed men "never consider God at all unless compelled to."[5]

WHY DOES CHRIST BID SINNERS TO COME?

In Matthew 11:25, Jesus says, "I praise You, Father, Lord of heaven and earth, that You have hidden these things from the wise and intelligent and have revealed them to infants." Why?

He's saying that God decides who will receive the truth. He has determined to hide it from the wise and intelligent, but to reveal it to babes. Why did God do that? Verse 26 explains, "Yes, Father, for this way was well-pleasing in Your sight." He withholds the truth from some and reveals it to others because it pleases Him to do so. Then verse 27 continues, "All things have been handed over to Me by My Father; and no one knows the Son except the Father; nor does anyone know the Father except the Son, and anyone to whom the Son wills to reveal Him."

It's very clear: *You're not going to believe unless God wills it.* You're not going to come alive unless God raises you. You're not going to understand truth unless God reveals it to you. And yet, verse 28 includes Christ's open invitation, "Come to Me, all who are weary and heavy-laden, and I will give you rest." What an amazing thing. This is a constant, apparent paradox in Scripture.

People often ask me, "How do you resolve that?" I don't. I have no idea how to resolve that. The offer to come to Christ is made universally, but the power to come is limited to those whom the Father raises.

We cannot know whom the Father will draw to Himself until He draws them. But that's partially the source of the hope and fervor in our evangelism. We don't know whom He has elected unto salvation, so we plead with *all sinners* to repent and believe, while fully recognizing that it is only God's work that regenerates the dead heart and gives spiritual life.

You're not going to find a text of Scripture in which Jesus defends the ability of sinners. You'll never find a text where He defends the freedom of the human will. Jesus is no Arminian. All those Scriptures we went through and many, many more place all the work of salvation on God's side. It is all His will and His power, not ours.

THE DEADNESS OF THE HEART

To further explain the inability of fallen mankind, I want to take a deeper look at what it means to be the living dead. First of all, the Bible has a lot to say about the deadness of the human heart. Several verses in the Old Testament show this reality.

All the way back in Genesis 6, Scripture defines the whole human race after the Fall. Verse 5 says, "The Lord saw that the wickedness of man was great on the earth, and that every intent of the thoughts of his heart was only evil continually." The biblical diagnosis of every human heart is that it *only produces evil continually*. It creates nothing but evil.

Jeremiah 17:9, a verse you may have memorized, declares, "The heart is more deceitful than all else and is desperately sick." Psalm 143:2 adds, "No man living is righteous." And Proverbs 20:9 asks, "Who can say, 'I have cleansed my heart, I am pure from my sin'?" The implied answer is nobody. *Nobody* can say, "I got my act together. I cleansed my own heart. I made the right choice."

Jeremiah 13:23 asks the same question this way: "Can the Ethiopian change his skin or the leopard his spots?" The prophet then answers, "Then you also can do good who are accustomed to doing evil."

When you look at the biblical diagnosis of the human heart, there's nothing in there that can or will respond correctly to the truth. It is desperately wicked, and what proceeds out of that heart is all the sins and iniquities that characterize it (Matt 15:19). You could find many other passages that confirm this truth about the sinful heart (e.g., Ezek 36:26; Mark 7:21–23; Luke 6:45; Rom 1:21; Eph 4:18; Heb 3:12).

THE DEADNESS OF THE MIND

A second aspect of the fallen condition explained in Scripture is the mind. Romans 1:28 says, "God gave them over to a depraved mind," which is a mind that doesn't function. So the unregenerate have nonfunctioning minds when it comes to spiritual truth. Furthermore, 2 Corinthians 4:4 says, "The god of this world has blinded the minds of the unbelieving so that they might not see the light of the gospel of the glory of Christ." Not only is the unbelieving mind corrupted by sin, it is also blinded by Satan.

Paul elaborates on this in Romans 8:5, "Those who are according to the flesh set their minds on the things of the flesh, but those who are according to the Spirit, the things of the Spirit." If you're living according to the flesh, then your mind is devoted to the flesh. Verse 6 adds, "The mind set on the flesh is death." Here again, as we've seen in so many verses already, Paul speaks of unregenerate people in terms of "death." Finally, in verse 7, Paul says, "The mind set on the flesh is hostile toward God; for it does not subject itself to the law of God, for it is not even able to do so." The human mind is spiritually dead and has absolutely no ability or desire to choose God. In fact, the opposite is true. The mind is hostile to God.

Ephesians 4:17–19 gives another vivid description of the miserable state of fallen humanity. Paul instructs his readers to

> walk no longer just as the Gentiles also walk, in the futility of their mind, being darkened in their understanding, excluded from the life of God because of the ignorance that is in them, because of the hardness of their heart; and they, having become callous, have given themselves over to sensuality for the practice of every kind of impurity with greediness.

The unbelieving mind is so corrupted by sin that it is useless. It's so scarred over by sin that it can no longer differentiate truth from error. It is characterized by "futility" and is "excluded from the life of God"—it's as good as dead in its ability to recognize and respond to God's truth.

Paul adds in Titus 1:15, "To those who are defiled and unbelieving, nothing is pure, but both their mind and their conscience are defiled." Every biblical description is the same: The unregenerate mind is ignorant, dark, defiled, futile, empty, and dead. No matter where you turn in Scripture, the biblical portrait of the unregenerate mind is bleak.

One more significant passage—which we could say much about—is 1 Corinthians 2:14, "A natural man does not accept the things of the Spirit of God, for they are foolishness to him; and he cannot understand them, because they are spiritually appraised." The things of God are spiritually discerned—which poses a massive problem for the sinner because he is *spiritually dead*. This is why Paul says the sinner "does not" and "cannot" accept spiritual truth. Because his mind is utterly corrupted by sin, he is unwilling and unable to do so.

THE DEADNESS OF THE WILL

Some people might still attempt to argue that down deep in mankind, the will is still able to choose Christ. But consider Christ's words in John 8:44, "You are of your father the devil, and you want to do the desires of your father. He was a murderer from the beginning, and does not stand in the truth because there is no truth in him. Whenever he speaks a lie, he speaks from his own nature, for he is a liar and the father of lies."

As an unredeemed sinner, all of that applies to you. You have a father, the devil, and you *want* to do his desires—and he's a murderer and a liar who hates the truth. You have no desire for the truth because you want to do the desires of the devil (cf. Eph 2:2). So when Scripture speaks the truth, you don't believe it. You wouldn't want to even if you could, because your will is bent toward sin.

In his tremendous work *On the Bondage of the Will*, Martin Luther explains,

> Satan is the prince of the world, and, according to the testimonies of Christ and Paul, rules the wills and minds of those men who are his captives and servants.... [It] is plainly

> proved by scriptures neither ambiguous nor obscure—that Satan, is by far the most powerful and crafty prince of this world; (as I said before,) under the reigning power of whom, the human will, being no longer free nor in its own power, but the servant of sin and of Satan, can will nothing but that which its prince wills. And he will not permit it to will anything good: though, even if Satan did not reign over it, sin itself, of which man is the slave, would sufficiently harden it from willing good.[6]

Paul puts it this way in Romans 6:20: "You were slaves of sin." The unredeemed person is not free to live righteously. He is a slave of sin, unable to change his sin-bound will. Just as sinners will not be raised from the dead unless God raises them, they will not be free from the slavery of sin unless God frees them (John 8:36).

Out of a dead heart, mind, and will comes only that which pleases the father of the living dead, Satan. So again, we read in Mark 7:20–23, "That which proceeds out of the man, that is what defiles the man. For from within, out of the heart of men, proceed the evil thoughts, fornications, thefts, murders, adulteries, deeds of coveting and wickedness, as well as deceit, sensuality, envy, slander, pride and foolishness. All these evil things proceed from within and defile the man."

THE TRIAL OF THE DEAD

There's one final text that perfectly sums up man's deadly situation—Romans 3:9–18. In case someone still believes there is something in unregenerate man that allows him to pursue what is right, Paul gives one of the clearest arraignments of mankind's wretchedness found in all of Scripture.

> What then? Are we better than they? Not at all; for we have already charged that both Jews and Greeks are all under sin; as it is written, "There is none righteous, not even one; there is none who understands, there is none who seeks for God; all have turned aside, together they have become useless; there is none who does good, there is not even one." "Their throat is an open grave, with their tongues they keep deceiving," "the poison of asps is under their lips"; "whose mouth is full of cursing and bitterness"; "their feet are swift to shed blood, destruction and misery are in their paths, and the path of peace they have not known." "There is no fear of God before their eyes."

First, in verse 9, he states that "both Jews and Greeks are all under sin." By including Jews and Gentiles, Paul is simply saying that all mankind is in view. They belong to the same sin-cursed family. The word "under" is translated from the common Greek preposition *hupo*. The idea here is that all mankind is under the power, authority, and dominion of sin. "The whole world lies in the power of the evil one" (1 John 5:19). The world is like a baby, cradled asleep in the arms of the devil. This is a dramatic and shocking picture, but it communicates the point that every human being is under the dominion of sin and Satan.

Following this comprehensive condemnation in verse 9, Paul gives a string of quotes taken from the Old Testament to solidify his universal diagnosis of unredeemed hearts. He writes, "As it is written 'There is none righteous'" (v. 10). Some readers would instinctively insert here, "Except me." Paul quickly closes the door on such self-righteousness by adding the words, "Not even one." This is the first of thirteen indictments Paul provides in Romans 3—no one is righteous.

The concept of righteousness is the theme of Romans in many ways. It's a tremendously important idea which appears frequently throughout the book. The word "righteous" simply means good and just. Paul's point is that absolutely no one qualifies as either just or good. But how good does a person have to be, to be considered truly "righteous"? Scripture doesn't leave room for levels of righteousness—there's no grading curve or tier system that softens the blow. God's Word is unequivocal: You are either perfectly righteous, or you are entirely unrighteous.

Jesus makes this point in Matthew 5:48, "You are to be perfect, as your heavenly Father is perfect." This is an unachievable standard—and that's the point. We have to recognize that we can only reach this standard through the righteousness of Christ. Believers are not justified by their own righteousness (Phil 3:9), but by the imputation of Christ's righteousness, which is perfect (2 Cor 5:21). The perfect righteousness of Christ includes not only His satisfaction of the penalty of the law on the cross, but also His perfect obedience to God's law throughout His life (Matt 3:15; Rom 5:19). This is what theologians refer to as Christ's *active obedience*. And it means that Christ's perfect obedience to the law is imputed to believers so that before God they are declared to be as righteous as Christ.

Without the imputation of Christ's righteousness, all mankind stands condemned before God. As Paul sums up, "There is none righteous, not even one" (Rom 3:10). This is the state of every person, before faith in Christ.

Paul adds a second indictment in verse 11, "There is none who understands." Here he is quoting from Psalms 14:2 and 53:3. His point is that man is not only evil, he's also ignorant, which compounds his problem. Not only is man utterly bad, he doesn't even understand what good is. As we've already seen, Paul explains that the natural man does not accept spiritual truth (1 Cor 2:14). He can't know it because it is spiritually discerned, and in the flesh he is spiritually dead.

As a third indictment, Paul continues in verse 11, "There is none who seeks for God." Someone might ask: What about those passages of Scripture that speak about seeking God, like 2 Chronicles 7:14 or Jeremiah 29:13? But the reality is that you can't seek Him until He has already found you. Scripture is clear that we love God because He first loved us (1 John 4:19). Here in Romans 3, Paul is saying, "There's none who seeks after God *by his own ability*." This echoes the truth we've already seen in John 6:44, that "no one can come to Me unless the Father who sent Me draws him." The people who truly seek God do not seek Him on their own initiative.

In verse 12, Paul offers a fourth indictment, "All have turned aside." Men don't follow God's path. As Isaiah writes, "All of us like sheep have gone astray, each of us has turned to his own way" (Isa 53:6). Proverbs 14:12 adds, "There is a way which seems right to a man, but its end is the way of death." Without exception, all men have gone off track.

Continuing this thought in verse 12 of Romans 3, we see a fifth indictment, "Together they have become useless." The Greek term basically means that unregenerate man is good for nothing. The human race can't serve its intended function. Fallen humanity is like salt without savor, rotten fruit, or milk that's gone bad. They have no more value; they're good for nothing.

The sixth indictment from this passage is in the final lines of verse 12, "There is none who does good, there is not even one." In verse 10 Paul says, "There is none righteous, not even one." He's expanding on that same point here, showing the extent of man's corruption. Not only is there no one who *is* good—here the apostle says there is no one who even *does* good. This is a condemnation of fallen mankind's character. He doesn't do anything that is good in the sense that it has eternal value and glorifies God. He *can't*.

Man's inability to do good will inevitably manifest itself in his speech. This is why Paul adds a seventh indictment in verse 13, "Their throat is an open grave." This is a disgusting picture. In the ancient world, nothing was more abominable than an open grave and a stinking, rotting body putting out its revolting stench. Paul isn't merely talking about bad breath here—he's identifying something far worse.

A man's soul is dead in trespasses and sin, and its putrefying decay emits a foul and filthy odor through his throat in the form of wicked words. His mouth becomes a vent for the corruption of his soul. As Jesus said in Matthew 15:18, "The things that proceed out of the mouth come from the heart, and those defile the man." Proverbs 15:28 likewise explains, "The mouth of the wicked pours out evil things." The true revealer of a corrupt character is the mouth. Man's depravity spills out in his foul speech.

Paul moves from the throat to the tongue to add an eighth indictment in verse 13, "With their tongues they keep deceiving." The verb for "deceiving" is in the imperfect tense to indicate a continuous habit. David wrote that "the words of [the ungodly] are wickedness and deceit" (Ps 36:3). The Old Testament is loaded with statements about the corruption of the mouth. In Psalm 5:9 David bemoans, "There is nothing reliable in what they say; their inward part is destruction itself." Speaking again of the wicked, he writes, "Your tongue devises destruction, like a sharp razor, O worker of deceit. You love evil more than good, falsehood more than speaking what is right" (Ps 52:2–3). Solomon likewise warned of the evil unleashed by the sinner's tongue: "The tongue of the wise makes knowledge acceptable, but the mouth of fools spouts folly" (Prov 15:2). Describing the sinful state of those separated from God, Isaiah writes, "Your hands are defiled with blood and your fingers with iniquity; your lips have spoken falsehood, your tongue mutters wickedness" (Isa 59:3). And the prophet Jeremiah wrote, "'They bend their tongue like their bow; lies and not truth prevail in the land; for they proceed from evil to evil, and they do not know Me,' declares the LORD" (Jer 9:3).

Paul describes the evidence of man's depravity that pours forth from his throat and tongue, and closes verse 13 with a ninth indictment. He writes, "The poison of asps is under their lips." This is a quotation from Psalm 140:3, where the psalmist draws an analogy with a snake. The fangs of a viper fold up into its jaw until it strikes. Then the fangs come down, and sacks of venom "under their lips" force poison through the fangs and into the prey. Words are likewise deadly, and they expose the deadness of the human heart.

Moving into verse 14, Paul includes a tenth indictment concerning the whole mouth, "Whose mouth is full of cursing and bitterness." This line is taken from Psalm 10:7. "Cursing" is simply to speak evil of someone. "Bitterness," from the Greek *pikria*, has to do with extreme wickedness which results in vile speech against God and man (cf. Eph 4:31). It's not hard to find evidence of Paul's claim—all you have to do is listen to how the world talks. Our culture is dominated by speech that is foul, bitter, angry, cursing, filthy, blasphemous, proud, lustful, violent, lying, deceptive, and destructive. Psalm 64:3 describes wicked men as those "who have sharpened their tongue like a sword. They aimed bitter speech as their arrow." Like an open grave, the throat, tongue, lips, and mouth reveal the stench of a depraved heart.

The apostle shifts his focus in verse 15 but continues with the anatomical imagery. He moves from the mouth that depicts fallen man's conversation, to the feet, which display fallen man's conduct. Paul's eleventh indictment reads, "Their feet are swift to shed blood." This quotation is taken from Isaiah 59:7, and it's a clear reference to sinful man's murderous tendencies. Mankind kills their own at a greater rate than any animal does. We are murderers, whether we're talking about mass genocide, cannibalism, or national conquest. The history of man is a history of massacre. The idea that man is basically good is nonsense. The natural man is a bloodthirsty killer.

You may object at this point because you have never personally murdered anyone. But we have to remember that not all men are as bad as they could be. You're not as bad as some people, but you are still totally corrupted by sin. Even though some people are worse than others, no one is good according to *God's standard* of goodness.

Even if you have never killed anyone, 1 John 3:15 says, "Everyone who hates his brother is a murderer." So the only difference between murder and hate is the act itself. The attitude is exactly the same, and in God's eyes, the two sins are tantamount. Listen to the words of Jesus in Matthew 5:21–22,

> You have heard that the ancients were told, "You shall not commit murder" and "Whoever commits murder shall be liable to the court." But I say to you that everyone who is angry with his brother shall be guilty before the court; and whoever says to

> his brother, "You good-for-nothing," shall be guilty before the supreme court; and whoever says, "You fool," shall be guilty enough to go into the fiery hell.

Hating and cursing one another are morally equivalent to murder. Most people haven't murdered anyone, but people who are the children of the devil are characterized by hate. Ultimately, the hatred of the world begins with hatred for God. Remember that Jesus told His disciples, "If the world hates you, you know that it has hated Me before it hated you" (John 15:18). The hatred of the world is not shocking or mysterious. Unredeemed people living in the wicked system of the world will never choose to be saved by Christ because they hate Him.

Verse 16 takes this a step further with a twelfth indictment. Paul writes, "Destruction and misery are in their paths." The Greek word translated "destruction" (*suntrimma*) is a compound word with the meaning of shattering or breaking into bits. The abstract sense of "destruction" is "misery." "Misery" in this verse refers to the suffering which accompanies destruction. Men leave a trail of destruction and misery as they move through their lives—violence, bloodshed, and devastation mark all human history.

The thirteenth and final indictment comes in verse 17, "And the path of peace they have not known." Fallen humanity is not very good at keeping peace. Whether it's quarrels in personal relationships, crimes, revolutions, massive wars, or genocide, this is characteristic of man: He does not know peace.

These thirteen indictments by Paul make the universal state of unredeemed men clear. Paul even says "*all* [are] under sin" in verse 9 to remove any doubt that this passage refers to the entirety of the human race. I should add that Paul not only says "all" are under sin in verse 9, but he uses the word "none" four times and the word "all" three times throughout these thirteen indictments. These terms are universal terms; no human but Christ Himself is exempt from these indictments.

These nine verses in Romans give the basic diagnosis of all mankind: They are a whole race of Lazaruses, dead in sin. We are all born evil, selfish, and in love with our sin. We thrive on selfish lust and want to do the things that please our father, the devil. In this wicked state, we would never choose God.

But the Holy Spirit doesn't stop with this thirteen-part indictment.

In verse 18, He reveals the underlying attitude that motivates sinful man's behavior, "There is no fear of God before their eyes." Paul is quoting from Psalm 36:1. This is the key. The reason man is so abandoned to sin is because he does not fear God. To fear God means to have a respect for God. It isn't just the fear of His judgment; it's the desire to honor Him for His works. As Proverbs 16:6 says, "By the fear of the Lord one keeps away from evil."

But men universally do not fear God. They do not honor God. They do not glorify Him as God. Fearing God, in Scripture, is a synonym for being a true believer, a God-fearer. It describes that man or woman who has respect for God's holy work, Word, and will.

It is not the idea of panic or dread, but reverential respect and awe.

At the root of man's problem of sin and unrighteousness is a practical atheism—he does not fear God. All the previous indictments rise out of the absence of that fear. He is motivated by a wrong attitude toward God. The whole human race shares this attitude. That is why no one would choose God, even if they had the power to do so.

On sinful man's rejection of God, D. Martyn Lloyd-Jones writes,

> Why is it that man ever chooses sin? The answer is that man has fallen away from God, and as a result, his whole nature has become perverted and sinful. Man's whole bias is away from God. By nature he hates God and feels that God is opposed to him. His god is himself, his own abilities and powers, his own desires. He objects to the whole idea of God and the demands which God makes upon him.[7]

GOD'S GIFT TO THE DEAD

Some may object at this point, saying that human belief is necessary for salvation. It's true, of course, that we have to believe the gospel to be saved. But again, Ephesians 2:8 says, "For by grace you have been saved through faith; and that not of yourselves, it is the gift of God." Even faith has to be given to the spiritually dead. This truth is abundantly proven throughout Scripture.

Second Peter 1:1 says, "Simon Peter, a bond-servant and apostle of Jesus Christ, to those who have received a faith of the same kind as ours." All believers, Peter included, have faith only because we received it from God. It is a divine gift.

Philippians 1:29 is clear on this point as well. Paul writes, "To you it has been granted for Christ's sake, not only to believe in Him, but also to suffer for His sake." It has been granted to you, by God, for the sake of Christ, to believe and to suffer. If God didn't grant you the power to believe, you *couldn't* believe. Dead people can't respond to the gospel unless life and faith are granted to them. That's why the analogy of death is used.

In Acts 3, after Peter and John healed a lame man, verse 16 says, "On the basis of faith in His name, it is the name of Jesus which has strengthened this man whom you see and know; and the faith which comes through Him has given him this perfect health in the presence of you all." The man's faith to believe *in* Christ came to him *through* Christ. It didn't come from himself.

In Philippians 1:6 Paul writes, "I am confident of this very thing, that He who began a good work in you will perfect it until the day of Christ Jesus." Who began the good work in all believers? God initiated the work, because dead men have no ability to initiate anything. They're dead.

Second Timothy 2:25–26 says that we are to treat people gently "if perhaps God may grant them repentance leading to the knowledge of the truth, and they may come to their senses and escape from the snare of the devil, having been held captive by him to do his will." Repentance is a gift granted by God. Scripture is perfectly clear. The only way you can escape from the snare of the devil is to come to your senses. The only way you can come to your senses is to have the knowledge of the truth. But the only way you can have the knowledge of the truth is if God grants you repentance.

We have already shown that we are unable and unwilling to repent and believe in Christ. So if we are ever to repent and believe, it must be like it was for Lazarus. God who commands the dead to rise must also give us the power to repent and believe. The core of this great truth is that God must Himself give life to the dead. This is also known as *regeneration*. And regeneration is what theologians would call *monergistic*, which means that it is a work of God alone.

In regeneration, we are passive. God awakens us and grants us repentance and faith concurrently, to bring about salvation. If you don't believe that repentance and faith are gifts given by God, then there is no possibility for fallen men to be saved. How will they repent and believe unless God grants it to them? They certainly can't do it in their natural, fallen state.

That's why denying this doctrine creates problems for evangelism. Rejecting absolute inability and yet evangelizing is like standing on a bridge over rapids, watching somebody bob up and down screaming, and saying to them, "I have good news for you. If you can get yourself out of there, we'll dry you off. Come on, get out of there." He can't get out of the rapids by his own strength. You're offering him something that he's not capable of doing. The gospel call without the understanding that regeneration is a monergistic work of God makes no sense.

If regeneration is not a sovereign work of God, then He does no more for the believer than He has done for the multitudes that are now in hell. But is the difference between believers and unbelievers nothing more than their will to live? That would mean the real difference between believers and unbelievers has to do with *man's choice*, not God's, and that everybody in hell just didn't have the will to rescue themselves.

Hear these words from Titus 3:3–6,

> For we also once were foolish ourselves, disobedient, deceived, enslaved to various lusts and pleasures, spending our life in malice and envy, hateful, hating one another. But when the kindness of God our Savior and His love for mankind appeared, He saved us, not on the basis of deeds which we have done in righteousness, but according to His mercy, by the washing of regeneration and renewing by the Holy Spirit, whom He poured out upon us richly through Jesus Christ our Savior.

He saved us. Not because of anything we did, but because of His mercy.

Some people try to make regeneration a preliminary and separate work to conversion. The idea is that regeneration occurs, and then sometime after the new birth, full salvation comes. That can't be right. The word "regeneration" used in Titus 3:5, *palingenesias*, appears only here and in Matthew 19:28, where it has an eschatological sense. But Titus 3:5 is the only place in the Bible where the word "regeneration" is connected to salvation. Notice, though, that it is "the washing of regeneration and renewing by the Holy Spirit." Therefore, regeneration and washing are one and the same glorious reality.

You cannot be regenerated unless you've been washed. Therefore, regeneration and conversion must occur simultaneously. Salvation occurs at once, in one great miracle when we believe the Scripture (Jas 1:18). You believe the gospel because at that very moment you are regenerated, washed, converted, justified, and sanctified. Life is given all at once, just like it was for Lazarus—and out of the spiritual grave we come.

Because of this, all the glory goes to God alone, and we will spend the rest of our lives here and in eternity giving Him praise for raising us from the dead. "Oh, the depth," says Paul, "of the riches both of the wisdom and knowledge of God! How unsearchable are His judgments and unfathomable His ways!" (Rom 11:33).

HOPE FOR THE DEAD

This diagnosis of man has been the conviction of Christians through the centuries. Against Pelagius and Pelagianism, Augustine taught that no fallen man would choose God unless God first intervened by grace. Against Erasmus, Martin Luther defended this doctrine in his powerful treatise *On the Bondage of the Will*. Jonathan Edwards wrote *The Freedom of the Will* on the same topic. The Council of Dort and many other theological statements throughout history have affirmed this biblical truth.[8] As just one example, the Westminster Confession of Faith (1647) 6.4 says fallen man is "utterly indisposed, disabled, and opposite to all good, and wholly inclined to all evil." And as we have seen, the doctrine of man's absolute inability is rooted in Scripture itself.

So what can the sinner do? Well, he has only one option. He brings nothing, and he offers nothing. All he can do is cry out to God for mercy to save him. But the sinner, in order to do that, must have come to the true recognition of his sin under the prompting of the Holy Spirit, who has convicted him of sin, righteousness, and judgment (John 16:8). The sinner must have come to the end of himself so that he denies himself, and cries out to God for salvation which is a gift of grace. Until God moves, nothing changes.

We see this in 1 Corinthians 1:26, "Consider your calling, brethren." This "calling" is the effectual calling to salvation. Paul continues, "There were not many wise according to the flesh, not many mighty, not many noble." When the Lord started calling people to salvation, obviously He didn't choose the wise, mighty, or noble. Verses 27–28 explain, "God has chosen the foolish things of the world to shame the wise, and God has chosen the weak things of the world to shame the things which are strong, and the base things of the world and the despised God has chosen."

Three times, Paul repeats, "*God has chosen.*" Verse 29 explains why: "*So that no man may boast before God*" (emphasis added). So if you're a believer, you brought nothing to your salvation. You can't boast in your wisdom, your virtue, or your spirituality. You can boast only in God's power and grace.

That chapter concludes with these marvelous words: "By His doing"—by God's doing—"you are in Christ Jesus" (v. 30). You didn't get to a right standing with God by your own will. Your deadness in sin forbade that. "*By His doing* you are in Christ Jesus, who became to us wisdom from God, and righteousness and sanctification, and redemption, so that, just as it is written, 'Let him who boasts, boast in the Lord'" (vv. 30–31, emphasis added; cf. Jer 9:24).

The culmination of this passage is that God saves whom He chooses. The Spirit gives life, the Son sets free, and we contribute nothing, so that we forever give Him all the glory. The only thing the sinner can do is ask, like the man in Luke, "God, be merciful to me, the sinner!" (Luke 18:13).

As long as men try to hide the doctrine of depravity and take the offenses out of the gospel, they will disillusion people in the severest way. We have to be honest enough to give the bad news in order to deliver the good news that, though sinners can do nothing to overcome their sinfulness, Christ saves them by His grace alone.

That's the message of the gospel.

DIVINE ELECTION

"NO MAN CAN BE THOROUGHLY HUMBLED UNTIL HE KNOWS THAT HIS SALVATION IS UTTERLY BEYOND HIS OWN POWERS, DEVICES, ENDEAVORS, WILL, AND WORKS, AND DEPENDS ENTIRELY ON THE CHOICE, WILL, AND WORK OF ANOTHER, NAMELY, OF GOD ALONE."

MARTIN LUTHER[9]

A DISTURBING DOCTRINE

It's a well-established reality that the doctrine of election is disturbing to many people. In fact, it is not an overstatement to say there are people who hate the very thought of God's sovereign choice in salvation. Some have gone so far as to say that the doctrine is demonic.

To many, it seems unjust that God chooses who will be saved. It is such an affront to their personal sense of fairness that it causes them to question God's goodness. They find it emotionally unacceptable that He would decide whom He would save; that seems like an assault on free will and human choice—which many people are convinced is some kind of human right.

Thus, the conclusion of many believers is that the doctrine of divine election makes God unloving and unjust. Though many Christians who object to this doctrine may not express it in such sharp terms, that is the underlying sentiment—and it is pervasive in evangelicalism. Nor is that limited to those with minimal knowledge of the subject. Numerous ministry leaders, pastors, and major authors harbor animosity toward the doctrine of election.

IS GOD A MONSTER?

We must evaluate all of these claims in light of Scripture. But first, we must make it very clear that God is not to be measured by *our* understanding of what is right or just. We have to admit that our grasp of everything is warped in some way by our own sinfulness.

In Psalm 50:21, God said, "You thought that I was just like you." But He certainly is not. "'My thoughts are not your thoughts, nor are your ways My ways,' declares the Lord. 'For as the heavens are higher than the earth, so are My ways higher than your ways and My thoughts than your thoughts'" (Isa 55:8–9). This is the key: God has ways and thoughts that are incomprehensible, unresolvable, and inscrutable to us.

In the benediction from Romans 11:33–36, Paul affirms,

> Oh, the depth of the riches both of the wisdom and knowledge of God! How unsearchable are His judgments and unfathomable His ways! For who has known the mind of the Lord, or who became His counselor? Or who has first given to Him that it might be paid back to him again? For from Him and

> through Him and to Him are all things. To Him be the glory forever. Amen.

Who could know how God thinks? Who could be so bold as to tell God how He ought to think?

It is essential to understand that God is holy. He is infinitely and perfectly just. He is morally flawless and judgmentally perfect. Everything *in* Him and *of* Him and *for* Him and *from* Him and *by* Him is perfect. So we need to recognize from the outset that God does not adhere to any external standard of justice; rather, He *is* the standard. His will is just because *He* is inherently just. There is no standard to which He conforms; rather, it's our sense of justice that must conform to God.

The Puritan William Perkins had it right when he said we must not think that God does a thing because it is good and right, but rather that the thing is good and right because God does it.[10] The Creator owes nothing to the creature who cannot understand His ways, comprehend His mind, or be His counselor. In any case, how could God possibly be unjust for choosing to save some sinners that never deserved to be saved in the first place?

Instead of assuming that election is unjust or unfair based on our fallen sensibilities, we must turn to God's perfect Word to form our understanding of this pivotal doctrine.

GOD'S CHOICE IN THE OLD TESTAMENT

The doctrine of election did not suddenly materialize in the New Testament, as if it were alien to God's working throughout the Old Testament. After all, God chose Israel out of all the peoples in the world. God clearly chose Abraham, removed him from Ur of the Chaldees, and made him the father of a great nation. That's why Psalm 105:43 calls Israel "His chosen ones" and why Psalm 135:4 says, "The Lord has chosen Jacob for Himself."

Deuteronomy 7:6 and 14:2 say, "The Lord your God has chosen you to be a people for His own possession out of all the peoples who are on the face of the earth." God even said it wasn't because Israel was better or more attractive than any other people. He made it clear that *His own free will* was His only motivation in predetermining to set His love upon them, and no other reason (Deut 7:7–8). That is why He calls them "My elect" (Isa 45:4, NKJV).

God told Israel in Deuteronomy 10:14–15, "Behold, to the Lord your God belong heaven and the highest heavens, the earth and all that is in it. Yet on your fathers did the Lord set His affection to love them, and He chose their descendants after them, even you above all peoples, as it is this day." Moses's point here begins with the fact that the Lord owns everything. Everything in heaven and on earth belongs to Him. Yet out of it all, God chose the seed of Abraham and set His affection on them above all people. He made the choice. He passed by all the other nations. Election is no extraordinary act of God reserved for the New Testament era—it is how He has always operated. And the New Testament confirms that throughout in the language it uses.

GOD'S CHOICE IN THE GOSPEL AND ACTS

Beginning in Matthew 11:27, Jesus says, "All things have been handed over to Me by My Father; and no one knows the Son except the Father; nor does anyone know the Father except the Son, and anyone to whom the Son wills to reveal Him." The only way you'll ever know God the Father is if the Son wills to reveal Him to you, because that is *His* prerogative. No one knows the Father except the Son and whoever the Son wills to know Him.

Later, in Matthew 22:14 we read, "Many are called, but few are chosen." There's no way to state that any more clearly. A broad gospel call goes out to all, yet only a few are chosen by God to respond in faith.

That's why the church is explicitly called "the elect" and "the chosen." In Matthew chapter 24, during the Olivet discourse when our Lord is talking about the Second Coming, He says in verse 22, "Unless those days had been cut short, no life would have been saved; but for the sake of the elect those days will be cut short." Here our Lord uses "the elect" as a substantive—a noun that describes what believers are. They are "the elect," which simply means "the chosen" or "the selected."

Mark 13:20 makes it even more explicit. "Unless the Lord had shortened those days, no life would have been saved; but for the sake of the elect, *whom He chose*, He shortened the days" (emphasis added). There it is. Who chose whom? He chose us. In the time of the Tribulation there will be horrific judgments all over the world. But the time is condensed so the elect can survive. God does this, not for the sake of everybody, "but for the sake of the elect, whom He chose."

Continuing in Matthew 24, Jesus says in verse 24, "False Christs and false prophets will arise and will show great signs and wonders, so as to mislead, if possible, even the elect." They're not called "believers"; they're not called "Christians." They're called "the elect." In verse 31, Christ adds that when He returns, "He will send forth His angels with a great trumpet and they will gather together His elect." Here the church is called "His elect" because they are chosen *by Him*.

In Luke 18:7, the Lord asks, "Now, will not God bring about justice for His elect who cry to Him day and night?" Again, believers are called "*His* elect" because they are selected by Him.

Believers, then, are those whom God has chosen to belong to Him. In the Old Testament, admittedly, that select group was an earthly nation of people. In the New Testament, it is revealed that the elect are a spiritual cohort. That inescapable teaching fills the New Testament.

Moving on to the gospel of John, we read again of this glorious doctrine. Jesus says in John 3:3, "Truly, truly I say to you, unless one is born again he cannot see the kingdom of God." Nicodemus responds in verse 4, "How can a man be born when he is old? He cannot enter a second time into his mother's womb and be born, can he?" He's following the metaphor. He understands Jesus is speaking spiritually; he's just asking, "How can it happen?" And Jesus gives an astonishing answer.

Jesus doesn't say, "Well, you've got to pray this prayer and do this or that." He says, "Truly, truly, I say to you, unless one is born of water and the Spirit he cannot enter into the kingdom of God" (v. 5). Regeneration does not happen apart from the Holy Spirit. Christ continues in verses 6–7, "That which is born of the flesh is flesh, and that which is born of the Spirit is spirit. Do not be amazed that I said to you, 'You must be born again.'"

Whenever regeneration happens, wherever it happens, to whomever it happens—it is the work of the Holy Spirit. It is a birth from above.

In verse 8 Jesus explains, "The wind blows where it wishes and you hear the sound of it, but do not know where it comes from and where it is going; so is everyone who is born of the Spirit." You don't dictate where the wind goes. It goes wherever it pleases. So it is with the Spirit. He goes wherever He desires to go and works wherever He wants to work. He sovereignly does whatever He desires in whomever He desires. And in the end, He gets all the glory. Each believer's regeneration is based on divine election. It's the Spirit's choice, not ours.

Later, in John 15:16, Jesus tells His disciples, "You did not choose Me but I chose you." This is the consistent teaching of Scripture: The elect are chosen by God, not the other way around.

We are given similar truth in John 17. In verse 9 of this great, high-priestly prayer, Jesus says, "I ask on their behalf; I do not ask on behalf of the world, but of those whom You have given Me; for they are Yours." Jesus prays for only those whom the Father gave Him, and no one else. He is saying, "They belong to You, Father. You chose them. And You gave them to Me." We will return to examine this passage more closely later on, but for now the point is clear: *Certain people belong to God because He chose them.*

After the gospels, in Acts the biblical language continues to be unambiguous. For those who resist the doctrine of election, Acts 13:48 is a very hard verse to swallow. Paul and Barnabas were preaching the gospel; then Scripture says, "When the Gentiles heard this, they began rejoicing and glorifying the word of the Lord; and as many as had been appointed to eternal life believed." Only those who "*had been appointed* to eternal life believed." Only the chosen believe.

GOD'S CHOICE IN THE EPISTLES

This wonderful reality is clear not only in the gospel narratives but also throughout the epistles.

IN PAUL'S WRITING

We see the language of election used regularly in Romans. Paul teaches that we have been declared righteous (Rom 3:28), that the righteousness of God has been imputed to us through faith in Christ (4:22–25), and that those of us who have been redeemed, regenerated, and reconciled now belong to God (5:1). Then, verse 33 of Romans 8 says, "Who will bring a charge against God's elect? God is the one who justifies"—and since God declares that His elect are righteous before Him, no one can successfully bring an accusation against us.

Just as in Matthew 24, the church is called "*God's* elect." It's not that we elected God; it is that God elected us. Paul says this clearly in Colossians 3:12 by referring to believers as "those who have been chosen of God"; a literal translation of the Greek (*eklektoi*) shows that Paul says we are "the elect of God."

In Romans 9, God's Word continues to be both insistent and unmistakable on the doctrine of election. We could start with Jacob and Esau in verses 11–13, "Though the twins were not yet born and had not done anything good or bad, so that God's purpose according to His choice would stand, not because of works but because of Him who calls, it was said to [Rebekah], 'The older will serve the younger.' Just as it is written, 'Jacob I loved, but Esau I hated.'" Before they were ever born and before they had ever done anything good or bad, God chose to love one twin and hate the other. He determined that the older would serve the younger solely based on His purpose. God is the one who calls—that is absolutely clear. God made that choice before these brothers were even born.

At this point, we can easily identify with the questions in verse 14, "What shall we say then? There is no injustice with God, is there?" The setup may seem unfair to us. But Paul objects, "May it never be!"—*mē genoito*, the strongest negative in the Greek. This is the equivalent of Paul saying, "No, no, no! It's unthinkable!" It is impossible that any of God's actions could be called unjust.

Paul adds that sovereign election is nothing new for God. To make this kind of choice between people is the way He has always operated. Paul shows this in verse 15 by quoting God's words to Moses back in Exodus 33:19, "I will have mercy on whom I have mercy, and I will have compassion on whom I have compassion."

Romans 9:16 continues, "So then it does not depend on the man who wills or the man who runs, but on God who has mercy." That is to say, God's choice does not depend upon the will or the work of any man, but on God alone. And verse 18 adds, "So then He has mercy on whom He desires, and He hardens whom He desires." The truth of God's election is absolutely inescapable.

Shortly after this, in Romans 11, Paul uses the illustration of Elijah and the prophets of Baal to further his point. Elijah disgraced and defeated the prophets of Baal but then began to feel like he was the only faithful Israelite left (v. 3). Paul summarizes the divine response to the prophet's despair in verse 4: "I have kept for Myself seven thousand men who have not bowed the knee to Baal." Verse 5 explains, "In the same way then, there has also come to be at the present time a remnant according to God's gracious choice." God chose them, and God kept them.

In Elijah's day there were seven thousand Israelites who remained true to God, though they were unknown to His prophet. There is in every generation a remnant according to God's gracious choice. That's why Paul says of his own generation in verse 7, "Those who were chosen obtained [salvation], and the rest were hardened." Only *those who were chosen* obtained it. Those who weren't chosen were hardened. God actually "gave them a spirit of stupor" with "eyes to see not and ears to hear not" (v. 8). This is strong language about divine choice.

Continuing through the New Testament, we come to 1 Corinthians 1:26, "Consider your calling, brethren, that there were not many wise according to the flesh, not many mighty, not many noble." Just consider your church. How many of the world's wise are there? How many of its mighty and noble? How many earthly monarchs are in your church?

Paul adds in verses 27–29, "But God has chosen the foolish things of the world to shame the wise, and God has chosen the weak things of the world to shame the things which are strong, and the base things of the world and the despised God has chosen, the things that are not, so that He may nullify the things that are, so that no man may boast before God."

God receives all the glory. And it served God's glory best for Him to choose the foolish, the weak, and the despised of the world so that they couldn't possibly boast before Him. All the glory is His, as this passage repeats three times (vv. 26–28).

If the weak and the foolish chose God, this passage doesn't make any sense. If the weak and the foolish chose God, who gets the credit? They do. It turns the whole passage into nonsense. Besides, verse 30 states, "By [God's] doing you are in Christ Jesus." You and I are only in Christ because God made it so—He alone can claim the credit. To add emphasis to that point, verse 31 concludes, "Let him who boasts, boast in the Lord."

If you're dealing with someone who doesn't like the doctrine of election, this passage stops them cold in their tracks. But Paul has much more to say concerning this glorious reality.

In Ephesians 1:3, Paul writes, "Blessed be the God and Father of our Lord Jesus Christ, who has blessed us with every spiritual blessing in the heavenly places in Christ." How is it that we have been blessed? Verse 4 tells us, "Just as He chose us in Him before the foundation of the world, that we would be holy and blameless before Him." That is the reason.

God chose us in Christ before the foundation of the world, that we should be holy and blameless before Him when we're glorified. Verses 5 and 6 continue this train of thought: "He predestined us to adoption as sons through Jesus Christ to Himself, according to the kind intention of His will, to the praise of the glory of His grace, which He freely bestowed on us in the Beloved."

Paul's language leaves no room for us to claim any credit for ourselves. In love we were predestined to be adopted as sons through Christ. All of this because of the kind intention of God's own uninfluenced, holy, and sovereign will, so that in the end all the praise and glory goes to Him for His grace freely bestowed on us.

Even when Paul does praise his readers, he ultimately ties their good works and faithfulness back to God's initial work in salvation. In 1 Thessalonians 1:2–3, Paul writes, "We give thanks to God always for all of you, making mention of you in our prayers; constantly bearing in mind your work of faith and labor of love and steadfastness of hope in our Lord Jesus Christ in the presence of our God and Father." However, their faithfulness isn't a credit to them but an outworking of their identity: "Knowing, brethren beloved by God, His choice of you" (v. 4). They were the chosen. They were the elect. And that reality was evident to Paul from the way they lived their lives.

In 2 Thessalonians 2:13, Paul again says, "We should always give thanks to God for you, brethren beloved by the Lord, because God has chosen you from the beginning for salvation through sanctification by the Spirit and faith in the truth." Paul didn't congratulate the Thessalonians for being wise enough to come to Jesus—he thanked God for choosing to save them. Paul knew that God alone had redeemed them, and that the fruit in their lives was the result of His saving and sanctifying work. "It was for this He called you through our gospel, that you may gain the glory of our Lord Jesus Christ" (v. 14). All of this language in the New Testament is perfectly consistent in driving home the inescapable truth: If you are saved, God chose you in the past; He called you with a powerful, effectual call that awakened you from the dead; and He granted you clear understanding of the gospel and the gift of saving faith.

In light of this doctrine, Paul says in 2 Timothy 2:10, "For this reason I endure all things for the sake of those who are chosen, so that they also may obtain the salvation which is in Christ Jesus." Life was difficult and dangerous for Paul, which is illustrated by the metaphors he uses to describe his ministry. In verse 3, he fights like a soldier. He competes, in verse 5, strenuously like an athlete. He labors, in verse 6, like a hardworking farmer. In verse 9 he talks about the hardships he suffered, "even to imprisonment as a criminal." Why? "For this reason I endure all things *for the sake of those who are chosen*" (emphasis added). God has chosen some people for salvation, and Paul labored for their sake.

THROUGHOUT OTHER NEW TESTAMENT AUTHORS

The doctrine of divine election is not merely a point of emphasis for Paul—the other New Testament authors consistently speak of God's sovereignty in salvation. James 1:17 says, "Every good thing given and every perfect gift is from above, coming down from the Father of lights, with whom there is no variation or shifting shadow."

Everything that's good comes from God—and salvation would be at the top of the list. So in verse 18 James adds, "In the exercise of His will He brought us forth by the word of truth, so that we would be a kind of first fruits among His creatures." He did it, not us. Salvation came down from heaven as an exercise of His will. "*He* brought us forth," and He did it "by the word of truth," that is, through the gospel.

Shortly after this, James simply asks, "Listen, my beloved brethren: did not God choose the poor of this world to be rich in faith and heirs of the kingdom which He promised to those who love Him?" (2:5). Over and over, God's work in election is identified as the sole means of the salvation of His people.

Peter begins his first epistle on a similar note. "Peter, an apostle of Jesus Christ, to those who reside as aliens, scattered throughout Pontus, Galatia, Cappadocia, Asia, and Bithynia, who are chosen" (1 Pet 1:1).

Finally, in Revelation 13:8 and 17:8, Scripture says the names of believers were written down in the Lamb's Book of Life before the foundation of the world. This was a decision that God Himself made before anyone else even existed.

There is no way to conclude from all this clear biblical revelation that Scripture is ambiguous about God's sovereignty in electing sinners unto salvation. Yet throughout my own lifetime, I've answered questions about it, discussed and debated it both privately and publicly, myriad times. I have often said that if you believe the Bible, you believe in predestination and election. If you believe the Bible, you believe that God alone chose who would be saved—that He alone effectually calls them, grants them faith, and will one day complete His redemptive plan by perfecting and glorifying them in heaven.

Yet despite all the clarity we've seen so far, there are Christians who resist this doctrine.

ILLUSTRATING ELECTION

How does God handle such resistance? For the answer, we can look to Romans 9. We saw earlier that Paul talks about Jacob and Esau starting in verse 10—how God determined to love one and hate the other before either was even born. Then in verse 19 the apostle launches into a defense of election, arguing against a hypothetical objector.

Paul's imaginary opponent objects, "Why does He still find fault? For who resists His will?" (v. 19). If salvation was determined by divine choice before the first man was even born, then how can God find fault with anybody who rejects it? If it all depends on God being merciful to whom He will and compassionate to whom He will, how can people be held responsible? "How can God blame me if I don't believe? Wasn't it His will that I don't believe?" That's the natural response of prideful, unrepentant men. And Paul anticipated it.

Verse 20 gives an amazing response: "On the contrary, who are you, O man, who answers back to God?" Paul is saying, "Shut your mouth. Who do you think *you* are? How dare *you* accuse God of unjust condemnation? Are you fit to sit in judgment of your Creator?"

Paul then unleashes an illustration that emphasizes the futility of man's objections to election. "The thing molded will not say to the molder, 'Why did you make me like this,' will it?" (v. 20). When a potter makes a pot, the pot doesn't talk back. The pot doesn't say, "I don't want to be this shape; make me another shape. This isn't fair. I'd like to be like this or that pot, or some other pot."

Verse 21 raises another rhetorical question: "Or does not the potter have a right over the clay, to make from the same lump one vessel for honorable use and another for common use?"

It boils down to this: God is the potter; you are the clay. You have no right whatsoever to question your Maker. The clay is inanimate dirt; it is in no way comparable to the potter. And as vast as the gulf is between pot and potter, vaster still is the gulf between you and God. The potter, according to verse 21, has a right over the clay to shape it as He wills.

GOD'S GLORY IN JUDGMENT

Verse 22 adds another powerful rhetorical question, "What if God, although willing to demonstrate His wrath and to make His power known, endured with much patience vessels of wrath prepared for destruction?" Doesn't God have a right to demonstrate His wrath? Isn't that part of His revealed glory? Can't God make His power known in His judgment, in His wrath, and in His condemnation?

Yes, He can.

God wants to display His wrath. Why? To demonstrate His glory—and His wrath is part of His glory. The entrance of sin into the world (and here's a theological answer to a lot of questions) was *necessary* so that God could manifest His wrath and His judgment because they are as much elements of God's glory as any other aspect of His nature.

God allowed sin to exist so that He might display His holy wrath. No sin, no wrath. No wrath, no revelation of the full nature of God's glory. Many people wonder why God permitted sin in the first place—I believe this verse supplies the answer.

That is to say, I understand what this passage teaches. I'll confess that my puny human mind cannot entirely grasp the fullness of God's redemptive will. But Scripture is clear in what it teaches, and I hold on to that by faith.

Paul tells us that God "endured with much patience vessels of wrath prepared for destruction" (v. 22), and He did so for the purpose of displaying His wrath and power.

But how?

First, in judging sin. We see the righteous wrath of God in His judgment on sin. And if you have any question about that, all you need to do is read the closing chapters of the book of Revelation, and you will see the power of God on vivid display. There is revealed the complete destruction of the world (Rev 20:11; 2 Pet 3:10), along with the fiery judgments that He brings upon mankind (Rev

20:14–15). Then Christ comes in final conquest, clothed in blood-soaked garments and riding a white horse out of heaven to take the earth for His own possession and establish His eternal and glorious kingdom (19:11–16). God dramatically displays His power in His judgment.

But notice how Romans 9:22 concludes. It flips into passive verbs. It says God endures these "vessels of wrath prepared for destruction" not that *He prepared* for destruction but that they *were prepared* for destruction.

The passive nature of the verb is an important indicator for us as to how God's work of election was done in eternity past. While God is the one accomplishing all the work described in verses 18–24, Paul draws a differentiation between the Lord's saving work of election and the judgment displayed in His wrath, or what theologians call *reprobation*.

The reality of reprobation is difficult for most Christians to comprehend, often because of the many misconceptions that surround the doctrine. *Biblical Doctrine: A Systematic Summary of Biblical Truth* provides this more detailed explanation of reprobation to help dispel some of those common misconceptions.

> The doctrine of reprobation is a difficult teaching to accept. It is not pleasant to contemplate the miseries of eternal suffering in and of themselves, let alone to consider that the God who is love and is by nature a Savior has sovereignly determined to consign sinners to such a wretched end. Because it so easily offends fallen

man's sensibilities, many Christians who embrace the doctrine of election nevertheless reject the doctrine of reprobation altogether. That is also the case because the doctrine is so easily and so often misunderstood. Because of that, it is necessary to state what precisely we do and do not believe concerning the doctrine of reprobation.

In the first place, reprobation is often wrongfully conflated with the doctrine of equal ultimacy. Equal ultimacy teaches that God's actions in election and reprobation are perfectly symmetrical, so that God is just as active in working unbelief in the heart of the reprobate as he is in working faith in the heart of the elect. It pictures God in eternity past contemplating all humanity as yet unfallen and morally neutral and arbitrarily deciding to work sin and unbelief in the reprobate in order to be justified in consigning them to eternal punishment. Though this is what many think of when they hear the terms *reprobation* or *double predestination*, it is a gross caricature of the biblical doctrine of reprobation that is utterly foreign to Scripture, repugnant to the love and justice of God, and an aberration of historic Calvinism that has been rejected throughout Reformed orthodoxy.

Instead, Scripture teaches an unequal ultimacy with regard to election and reprobation—that is, while God does indeed decree both the salvation of some and the damnation of others, there is a necessary asymmetry in these decrees. Such an asymmetry is observed in Romans 9:22–23, for example, where Paul uses the active voice to speak of God's involvement in election ("vessels

> of mercy, which he has prepared beforehand for glory") and the passive voice to speak of his involvement in reprobation ("vessels of wrath prepared for destruction"). When God chose some and not others for salvation, he regarded them not as morally neutral but as already-fallen creatures. That is not to say that they were already created and fallen, for God's decree is eternal and thus pretemporal. Rather, from eternity, before anyone had been created, God conceived of or contemplated all people in light of their fall in Adam and thus as sinful creatures. In the case of the elect, he actively intervenes—setting his love on them, determining to appoint Christ as their Savior and to send the Spirit to sovereignly quicken them from spiritual death unto new life in Christ. In the case of the nonelect, however, he does not intervene but simply passes them by, choosing to leave them in their state of sinfulness and then to punish them for their sin. While he is the efficient cause of the blessedness of the elect, he is not the efficient cause of the wretchedness of the nonelect; rather, he ordains them to destruction by means of secondary causes. Thus, the elect receive mercy, for they are not punished as their sins deserve, but the nonelect receive justice, for they are rightly condemned as their sins deserve. On neither ground can God be charged with unrighteousness, because all are guilty and because he is not obligated to show grace to any.[11]

The distinction between election and reprobation is seen in the contrast between verses 22 and 23 of Romans 9. Put simply, the reprobate are passively prepared for destruction. But verse 23 says God will "make known the riches of His glory upon vessels of mercy." Here the verbs are active. "He prepared" the vessels of mercy Himself, while He simply endures those that are fitted for destruction. God is active in the redemption of the elect, but He is passive in the hardening of the reprobate.

While reprobation is frequently a hurdle to the acceptance of God's sovereignty in salvation, it is far from the only objection to the doctrine of election. It is instructive to examine those other common objections, and to consider the answers Scripture provides.

OBJECTION: Don't People Have to Choose God?

Election and reprobation are, like so many other matters, incomprehensible—yet true because they're revealed in Scripture. Failures of understanding don't negate their truthfulness. I don't fully understand the Trinity; I can't comprehend what it means to be three persons and yet one being. Neither can I comprehend the virgin birth or the person of Christ—how can He be truly man *and* truly God? Such realities are beyond finite intellect.

I can understand what the Bible says about these matters of God's sovereign election. At the same time, I understand the Bible says in 1 Timothy 2:4 that God "desires all men to be saved and to come to the knowledge of the truth." I also know it says in 2 Peter 3:9 that God is "not wishing for any to perish but for all to come to repentance." And I know that it commands us to preach the gospel to every creature, and that the gospel itself is essentially a command

(Matt 28:19–20). While we usually speak of it as a gift or an offer, at its heart the gospel is a command to repent and believe in the Lord Jesus Christ (cf. Mark 1:15; Acts 2:38).

I also understand that Scripture teaches human volition because it says, "Choose for yourselves today whom you will serve" (Josh 24:15), and Jesus said, "Come to Me, all who are weary and heavy-laden, and I will give you rest" (Matt 11:28). Jesus wept over the city of Jerusalem, saying, "How often I wanted to gather your children together, just as a hen gathers her brood under her wings, and you would not have it!" (Luke 13:34). I know that God wept over a recalcitrant, rebellious, and unbelieving Israel through the eyes of Jeremiah (Jer 13:17).

I understand all of that, and so do you—and every word of it comes from Scripture. But at the very same time, with absolutely no contradiction—except in our perception—Scripture unfolds to us the mystery that no sinner is capable of understanding spiritual truth. Paul writes, "A natural man does not accept the things of the Spirit of God, for they are foolishness to him; and he cannot understand them, because they are spiritually appraised" (1 Cor 2:14). He adds, "The word of the cross is foolishness to those who are perishing" (1:18). No sinner is capable of understanding the gospel and repenting on his own.

In fact, as Acts 11:18 says, the only way a sinner could ever repent is *if God grants him repentance* (cf. Phil 1:29). Even believing is beyond the capability of human beings because John 1:12–13 says, "As many as received Him, to them He gave the right to become children of God, even to those who believe in His name, *who were born, not of blood nor of the will of the flesh nor of the will of man, but of God*" (emphasis added). Believing does not come by the will of man or of his flesh; it comes by God's will alone.

The Bible is clear that people, by their own will, are incapable of understanding gospel truth, repenting, and believing. Thus, the only way any sinner can be redeemed is by the supernatural work of God. God has to grant understanding, repentance, and faith. God has to overpower spiritual death and give life, overpower spiritual blindness and give sight, overpower spiritual ignorance and give truth, overpower the pervasive love of sin and replace it with a desire for righteousness.

If anyone is ever saved, it is because God overrules all of that person's normal, natural inabilities. That's why we say that salvation is all of God—yet it is never apart from or in violation of human will. The profound, unsearchable reality is that no one would ever choose Christ if God had not first chosen him. We are saved and we have life because God freely chose to give it to us.

I don't mind some tension in the doctrine of election. I don't mind the fact that the Bible also says, "Whosoever will" (Rev 22:17, KJV), and that Jesus wept over Jerusalem because they would not come to Him and receive life (Matt 23:37).

How do these realities fit together? Anyone who will come to Christ can come, and anyone who does come will be received. How does that work together with election? I don't know. But be comforted in not knowing, because that limitation proves our minds are not equivalent to God's.

Just because we believe that Jesus is God doesn't mean we don't believe He's a man. Because we believe that He was born of a human mother does not mean we don't believe He was born of God. Because the Father is not the Son does not mean that they are different gods. And because we believe in the doctrine of election does not mean we don't believe in human responsibility. These are apparent paradoxes we cannot resolve. The real danger lies in coming up with some rationalistic middle ground which overrides the truth stated in Scripture.

So we believe the doctrine of election, not because it is fully comprehensible to our human minds, but because it is the unmistakable teaching of Scripture.

OBJECTION:
Election Is Conditioned on Foreknowledge

Some, in an effort to rescue God from the seeming unfairness of divine choice, propose that election should be explained by "foreknowledge." Peter uses the word in 1 Peter 1, where he speaks of believers "who are chosen" (v. 1). Then in verse 2 he adds that the believers were chosen "according to the foreknowledge of God the Father."

People who object to the doctrine of election often attempt to redefine it, saying God, in His omniscience, looked down through the annals of history and saw who would have faith in Him. Then, based on that, God chose whom He would save. Many Christians believe and teach this concept of "foreknowledge."

But that forces the question: How are these dead sinners going to resurrect themselves in order to believe in God? How are those who are totally blind and totally dead going to come to the place where they make the decision for salvation?

The answer, of course, is that they *can't* do any of those things. "Can the Ethiopian change his skin or the leopard his spots? Then you also can do good who are accustomed to doing evil" (Jer 13:23).

If God simply sees in the future who's going to make that decision, then His election is not based on His own will—it's based on man's merit and ability to make the right choice. It's as if God says, "The good guys are going to choose me, so I'm going to choose them." Such an idea is completely incongruous with every verse we've looked at so far.

So how should we understand foreknowledge from the Bible? First Peter 1:2 says believers are chosen "according to the foreknowledge of God the Father." But verse 20 says Christ "was foreknown before the foundation of the world, but has appeared in these last times for the sake of you." So if foreknowledge in verse 2 means that God looks ahead and sees what's going to happen, then it must mean the same thing in verse 20.

But did God look down through history and say, "Oh, look at that. Christ is going to give His life. Well, if He's going to do that, I'll make Him the Savior"? Obviously foreknowledge can't mean that, because Jesus said He came not to do His own will but the will of His Father (John 6:38). That's why Christ is called "My chosen one" in Isaiah 42:1.

The word "foreknowledge" is translated from the Greek word *prognōsis*. We get our own familiar medical term from this Greek word. It involves a predetermined choice.

The Greek root in *prognōsis* is *ginōskō*, which indicates that "foreknowledge" refers to an intimate kind of knowing. Christ was known by God, intimately as the Savior, before the foundation of the world. This same idea is seen in the Old Testament. The Greek version of the Old Testament translates what God says to Israel in Amos 3:2 using a form of *ginōskō*: "You only have I known of all the families of the earth" (NKJV). Of course this does not mean that the Jews were the only people God knew about, but rather that He knew them in a unique way. This is also the kind of knowing that Genesis refers to when it says, "Cain knew his wife, and she conceived and bore Enoch" (Gen 4:17, NKJV). It doesn't mean he merely knew who she was. It means he had an intimate relationship with her, which produced a son. It was a shock that Mary was pregnant before any man had ever *known* her, as she says in Luke 1:34, "How can this be, since I do not know [*ginōskō*] a man?" (NKJV). Jesus makes a similar comment in John 10:27 using *ginōskō*: "My sheep hear My voice, and I know them." He's talking about an intimate love relationship.

Therefore, what we have in foreknowledge is a predetermined union. Just as the Father had a predetermined relationship with the Son that would bring Him to be the sacrifice for sin, so the Father had a predetermined relationship with those whom He chose to save. Foreknowledge is a deliberate choice. It's *fore*knowledge because it's before time. In eternity past, God predetermined to establish an eternal relationship with certain souls.

One other passage seals this case. Peter gets up in Acts 2:22–23 and preaches, "Jesus the Nazarene, a man attested to you by God with miracles and wonders and signs which God performed through Him in your midst, just as you yourselves know—this Man, delivered over by the predetermined plan and *foreknowledge* of God, you nailed to a cross by the hands of godless men and put Him to death" (emphasis added).

Peter says Christ was delivered according to "the predetermined plan ... of God." The word for "plan" in this verse is *boulē*, which is used in classical Greek for convened councils making decisions. This was a pre-decided course of action—and God determined it. "Predetermined" (Gk., *horizō*) is a perfect participle, so it speaks of a completed action with continuing results. The word *horizō*, from which we get *horizon*, speaks of the boundaries or limits that are marked out. God, then, pre-decided a course of action and marked off the boundaries of that action. This is "the predetermined plan."

Then Peter adds, "and foreknowledge of God." In this context, it is clear that "foreknowledge" and "plan" refer to the same reality. We know this because both words are governed by the same article in the Greek. So Christ was delivered over to crucifixion because of both God's plan and foreknowledge.

God did not simply have information about what was going to happen to Christ—He predetermined it. Scripture leaves no ambiguity on the nature of the relationship between foreknowledge and the doctrine of election.

OBJECTION:
God Neither Knows Nor Controls the Future

Other objectors of a more radical variety, in another effort to remove responsibility from God, say He can't choose people for salvation since He can't know the future. This idea is known as Open Theism. The reason God doesn't know the future, they say, is because nothing has happened yet. Frankly, they have thereby created an idol and rejected the true and living God. But for the sake of argument, let's look at how Scripture handles this objection.

Open Theism teaches that God, like everybody else, needs to read the morning paper to find out what's going on. God can't have chosen before time began, because He doesn't know what anyone will do until they do it. Open Theists try to get God off the hook by claiming He cannot know what does not exist.

But if that is true, how is it that Isaiah 46:10 says He knows "the end from the beginning"? What does that mean? How is it that Isaiah

41:21–22 and 44:7–8 say God's knowledge of the future is what distinguishes Him from false gods? Or how is it that throughout the Bible He foretells events centuries before they ever occur? For example, Isaiah 44:28 names Cyrus as the ruler who will build up Jerusalem. Yet Cyrus's name—and his very existence—depended on an unimaginably long and complex series of human decisions separating the prophecy from its fulfillment. God knew it all.

In 1 Kings 13:2, God predicts the birth of King Josiah three hundred years before the event. In 2 Kings 19:25, He states explicitly that He had planned the military victories of the Assyrians long before they ever took place.

God foretells the Egyptians' voluntary oppression of Israel in Genesis 15:13. He foretells Pharaoh's hardening of his heart against Moses in Exodus 3:19. He foretells the Israelites' rejection of Isaiah's message in Isaiah 6:9. He foretells the Israelites' rebellion after Moses's death in Deuteronomy 31:16. He foretells Judas's voluntary betrayal of Christ in John 6:70–71. This list could go on and on.

God knew all of that.

Open Theists weakly offer, "Well, God is really good at analyzing trends. He's good at predicting with accuracy what might happen because He understands how history flows and unfolds." That's absurd. We've just looked at prophetic events that are the results of millions of human choices.

But what makes the whole theory the most ridiculous is this: If God doesn't know the future, He didn't know Jesus was going to die. That's a massive problem.

This is where the whole of Open Theism goes down the proverbial drain. As we've just seen, Acts 2:23 says Jesus was "delivered over by the predetermined plan and foreknowledge of God." Did God plan Jesus' arrest? Did God plan Jesus' crucifixion? Did God plan all of that in detail? According to Acts 4:28, they did to Him exactly what God had predestined to take place.

If God does not exercise power over human beings and their actions, and if God does not control those actions to the fulfillment of His plan, or if God doesn't even have a plan because He doesn't know the future—then how did He know Jesus would end up on a cross?

If He doesn't know the future, how did He know the Jews would cooperate? Or the Pharisees? Or Pilate, or Judas? How did He know Judas would stick around long enough to betray Jesus? How could He have known any of that if He doesn't know the future?

If God doesn't know the future, then He didn't know that His Son was going to die for your sins. That's ridiculous. He not only knows the future; He ordains the future. One writer put it this way:

> The crucifixion of Jesus Christ, the hinge pin of history and the indispensable condition of our salvation, was most certainly not left up to the vagaries of human decision! It was ordained from the foundation of the earth, and it is impossible that it might

> not have occurred. The Bible nowhere suggests or even permits the interpretation that Judas, Caiaphas, Pilate, and the soldiers were unwilling pawns forced by God into the commission of a horrible crime. They acted freely, [and] in accordance with their own motives and purposes. Yet they did [exactly] what God's hand and plan had predestined should happen.[12]

God ordains it all. He knows the future because He has written it. All of the choices are His—and that certainly includes the choice of salvation for lost, dead, blind sinners.[13]

OBJECTION:
Election Isn't Fair

Even though Scripture teaches election so clearly, some still object that it isn't fair. Yet salvation never has been a matter of fairness. Besides, we don't want what's fair, do we? It would be fair for God to save *no one.* What we really want is grace, not fairness. Election is rooted in pure grace. We see this grace on display especially when God elects the least deserving.

In 1 Corinthians 1:26–29, a passage we briefly looked at already, Paul exhorts his readers,

> Consider your calling, brethren, that there were not many wise according to the flesh, not many mighty, not many noble; but God has chosen the foolish things of the world to shame

> the wise, and God has chosen the weak things of the world to shame the things which are strong, and the base things of the world and the despised God has chosen, the things that are not, so that He may nullify the things that are, so that no man may boast before God.

When God does His choosing, when He is gracious to whom He will be gracious and merciful to whom He will be merciful, it seems as if His grace stoops to the most undeserving of all, so that no one could boast. Verse 30 says, "But by His doing you are in Christ Jesus." If you are in Christ Jesus, that is solely by God's doing, none of yours. Thus, verse 31 concludes, "Let him who boasts, boast in the Lord."

The people who believe the gospel in the New Testament are the poor, the outcast, the ignoble, the weak, the prostitutes, and the tax collectors. God passes by the mighty, noble, religious, and educated. A few of them believe, but they are the exception.

Salvation is not a matter of fairness—it is a matter of *pure grace*. And God has chosen to give that grace to the seemingly most undeserving, so that His sovereignty would be displayed.

We must not let this doctrine become the victim of our corrupted, sinful minds and our self-centered, proud reasoning. Like every other biblical truth, we open the Bible and submit ourselves to what it says—even if it's painful at first. Hell is an acutely painful doctrine, but that doesn't change its reality. While our finite minds may find it hard to grasp, we set all of that aside and submit ourselves to the Word of God.

And amazingly, the deeper we delve into this great doctrine, the more precious it becomes to us. I want to demonstrate this by looking at a final biblical argument for the doctrine of election.

THE FATHER'S GIFT TO THE SON

In addition to all of the passages we have already walked through, John 6 gives a unique perspective on the doctrine of election. Jesus says in John 6:64, "'There are some of you who do not believe.' For Jesus knew from the beginning who they were who did not believe, and who it was that would betray Him," namely, Judas. Then verse 65 adds, "And He was saying, 'For this reason I have said to you, that no one can come to Me unless it has been granted him from the Father.'"

I don't know how much more clearly that could be said. You can't come to Christ unless God grants you the understanding, the repentance, and the faith. Salvation is a work of God alone. That leaves us with a very important question to answer: Why did God choose to rescue any sinners from His just judgment in the first place?

The answer is staggering. To understand why God did this, I want to work through some clear and relevant texts of Scripture. Let's start in Titus chapter 1, to grasp the big picture of this glorious doctrine of election.

At the beginning of his letter to Titus, Paul introduces himself in ways that are essential to his calling. He is "a bond-servant of God and an apostle of Jesus Christ" (Titus 1:1). In the large sense, he serves God. In the more specific sense, he serves God as an apostle of Jesus Christ. In discharging his service to God and his apostleship on behalf of Jesus Christ, a number of elements characterize his ministry. First of all, he says, "For the faith of those chosen of God," or as some translations put it, "For the faith of God's elect" (LSB; cf. KJV, ESV). So Paul's first statement is that God has called him into His service for the sake of the elect.

But Paul doesn't know who the elect are, since there is no way to pre-identify them—God's sovereign election is hidden. So he preaches the gospel everywhere he goes, knowing that the Lord will use him to bring the gospel to some of the elect, who will believe. This is what evangelism is, and this was the first aspect of Paul's ministry. The ministry of evangelism is to proclaim the gospel so that the elect can hear it and believe.

Then there's a second aspect to Paul's ministry. It begins with evangelism and moves toward edification. He says he is called by God to represent Jesus Christ not only in bringing the truth to the elect so they can hear it and believe, but also to those who believe he brings "the knowledge of the truth which is according to godliness" (v. 1). That's the second aspect.

Once people have believed, they must be taught the truth so they can grow in Christlikeness. You could say the first aspect of the apostle's ministry was salvation, and the second was sanctification.

He says, "I preach the gospel so the elect can hear it and believe, and then I teach the Word of God so that those who believe can learn the truth, which produces godliness."

Finally, there's a third aspect of ministry, and it's as true for all of us as it was for him. Verse 2 says, "In the hope of eternal life." The third aspect is that element of encouragement and hope that looks at future glory.

Summing it all up, he says, "First of all, I preach the gospel so the elect can hear it and believe. Then I teach the Word so that those who believe can grow in the knowledge of the truth into godliness. Then, I tell them that eternal life leads to eternal glory to come so that they can live in hope. Hope becomes their greatest comfort." So there was, in his ministry, an aspect of salvation, an aspect of sanctification, and an aspect of glorification.

But verse 2 is where I really want to focus. Titus 1:2 says that everything Paul just mentioned—from justification to sanctification to glorification—was "promised long ages ago." The Greek says, "Before time." Before time began, God promised that He would save, sanctify, and glorify believers. But the question is, before time began, *to whom* did He make this promise?

He certainly didn't promise it to any human being—none existed. Before time began is before day one of creation. He certainly didn't promise this to angels because angels are not involved in God's plan of salvation; there are holy angels who never fell, and there are fallen angels who will never be redeemed. So God didn't make any promise about salvation, sanctification, and glorification to angels. In fact, it's very likely that when this promise was made, the angels didn't exist yet, because they were created when everything else was created.

So we return to the question: To whom did God make this promise?

What Paul speaks of here has to be an *intra-Trinitarian promise*—God making a promise within the Trinity itself. Look with me at Paul's second letter to Timothy, and let's follow this path.

Second Timothy 1:9 says, "[God] has saved us and called us with a holy calling, not according to our works, but according to His own purpose and grace which was granted us in Christ Jesus *from all eternity*" (emphasis added). That's the exact same Greek phrase as in Titus 1:2.

I don't know why the translators in Titus 1:2 rendered it "long ages ago," but here they translate the very same phrase as "from all eternity." It refers to something "before time began." So before there was time, God promised to save, sanctify, and glorify sinners.

But *to whom* did He make that promise?

Second Timothy 1:9 says it "was granted ... in Christ Jesus." That is the key. The Father made a promise *to the Son*. The whole of salvation comes from God. It is all about His own purpose, and it is granted on behalf of Christ. What you have to understand, then, is this: At some point in eternity past, the Father said to the Son, "I will redeem sinners, and I will do so for You."

Why would the Father do that? Because He loves the Son and, as we'll see in John 17, the Son celebrates the mutual love that He has with the Father. The Father determines, in His eternal love within the Trinity, that He will express His love for the Son by giving the Son a gift, and that gift is a redeemed humanity. He gives His Son a bride.

In the ancient world, a father chose his son's bride. That was the father's responsibility. Here you have the divine pattern, as God determines that He will choose a bride for His Son. It's a way that the Father could express His love to His Son.

Follow that thought through the sixth chapter of John, which we looked at earlier. In verse 37, Jesus says, "All that the Father gives Me will come to Me." This statement is critical to our understanding of election. Every person who ever has been or ever will be saved is a gift from the Father to the Son, determined in eternity past. The Bible tells us that God wrote down the names of the elect in the Lamb's Book of Life, fully knowing even before the foundation of the world that the Lamb would be slain to pay the price for that redemption (cf. Rev 13:8).

Traditionally, the one who took the bride always paid a price to the bride's father. In this case, the Father had to give up His own Son, and the Son had to give up His own life to pay the purchase price for His bride—and every saved individual is a part of that bride.

The Old Testament saints, too, are part of the bride and will take up residence in the New Jerusalem, which comes down out of heaven as a bride adorned for her husband (Rev 21:9–10). The whole of redemptive history is about the Father pursuing a bride for His Son—a bride whose identity He determined and recorded before the foundation of the world, so that every person who comes to Christ is given to Him by the Father. This is a staggering and glorious truth.

In fact, John 6:44 agrees, "No one can come to Me unless the Father who sent Me draws him." You can't understand, repent, or believe on your own. It's what we see also in verse 65: "I have said to you, that no one can come to Me unless it has been granted him from the Father." Salvation is by divine grant alone.

So how is it that people are saved? God chooses His elect. Their names are written down in the Lamb's Book of Life before the foundation of the world. Every one of them is a personal gift from the Father to the Son. Then, back to verse 37, "All that the Father gives Me will come to Me." This is what theologians through the centuries have called *irresistible grace*. If you are chosen, if you are a gift from the Father to the Son, you will come to Christ.

You will be given understanding, repentance, and faith. Then verse 37 says, "And the one who comes to Me I will certainly not cast out." Is that because there is something inherently valuable in the sinner? No. It's one of modern evangelicalism's illusions that we are so wonderful God cannot resist us. That's not true at all.

The value is not in the gift; the value is in the giver. It's because the Son so perfectly loves the Father that whatever the Father gives the Son takes on infinite value—because of the giver, not the gift.

We instinctively understand that. Gifts given to us by people we love automatically take on a value far beyond their sticker price. So our value comes not from some inherent goodness; it is because we have been given to the Son by the Father that we become precious to the Son—who would never reject a gift from His Father.

Finally, in verses 39 and 40, Jesus adds, "This is the will of Him who sent Me, that of all that He has given Me I lose nothing, but raise it up on the last day. For this is the will of My Father, that everyone who beholds the Son and believes in Him will have eternal life, and I Myself will raise him up on the last day."

Do you see the redemptive storyline here? The Father chooses a bride and writes each name down. In time, as history unfolds, those whom the Father has chosen are given to the Son. As they repent and believe, the Son receives them; He never rejects them. And the Son never loses any of them, but raises them up on the last day. None of that is based upon value that is inherent to us. We *become* precious because the Son cherishes the gifts from His Father.

The same image comes to us again in John 17. Some have called this chapter the Holy of Holies of Scripture because it grants us a glimpse into the communion within the Trinity, and in particular between the Father and the Son. In John 17, Jesus is talking to the Father about us—His eternal bride, given to Him by the Father.

"I ask on their behalf," Jesus says; "I do not ask on behalf of the world, but of those whom You have given Me; for they are Yours" (v. 9). In this sense, the elect have been God's since they were chosen. They have always belonged to Him, and He gives them as gifts of love to the Son. Then the Son prays for them—not for the world, but only for those whom the Father has given Him.

Anticipating the cross, Jesus continues in verse 11, "I am no longer in the world; and yet they themselves are in the world, and I come to You. Holy Father, keep them in Your name, the name which You have given Me, that they may be one even as We are." This is a very deep moment in this prayer. "I'm about to leave," Jesus says, "and they're going to remain here. So I'm asking You, Father, to keep them just as I have kept them up to now."

He continues in verse 12, "While I was with them, I was keeping them in Your name which You have given Me; and I guarded them and not one of them perished but the son of perdition"—Judas, who never was actually saved. But here again, Christ states that the Father gave the redeemed to the Son. And you see that Jesus says, "I kept them, Father, because You gave them to Me."

Again, why all of this? Because we are precious. And why are we precious? Not because we're inherently any better than anybody else, but because we've been given to the Son as gifts of love from the Father. Verse 24 explains this further: "Father, I desire that they also, whom You have given Me, be with Me where I am, so that they may see My glory which You have given Me, for You loved Me before the foundation of the world."

What is the purpose of all of this? The Father has chosen to give to the Son a bride to love, serve, praise, and glorify the Son forever. Think about it from a very earthly analogy. It would be like a man saying to his wife, "I love you so much, I just don't know how to express that love, so I've collected a huge group of people who are going to spend all their time and energy following you wherever you go, serving and praising you. They'll be your own private 'Hallelujah' chorus—doing everything you desire them to do. Not only that, but they're going to reflect your glory by being as much like you as possible."

Now, that sounds wacky because we can't conceive of any human being deserving that kind of praise. But Christ does, and in the mind of the Father, He is worthy of a redeemed humanity that will fill the eternal heavens with praise and honor for the Son. They will be, as Revelation 5:12 pictures them, gathered around the throne of God forever crying out, "Worthy is the Lamb that was slain to receive power and riches and wisdom and might and honor and glory and blessing." All the redeemed will serve Christ and be made like Him, for they shall see Him as He is (cf. 1 John 3:2; Phil 3:20–21).

As much as glorified humanity can be like deity incarnate, we'll be like Christ. This is the way that one must understand election. This is what Paul calls in Philippians 3:14 "the prize of the upward call." Our prize is being called to look like Christ so we can reflect His glory. This is why He's called the *prōtotokos*—the premier one among many brethren (Rom 8:29). We will bear His image for eternity.

Redemptive history ends when the last name in the Book of Life is redeemed. Then it's over. And in the very end, the Father will have gathered the bride in total and presented her to His Son in that great final location, the New Jerusalem (Rev 21:2, 9). It will eternally be the city of the bride. And all the saints of all the ages will make up that redeemed humanity, and they'll honor the Lord Jesus Christ forever. That will satisfy the Father, who has expressed lavish and perfect love for the Son.

We are being saved, beloved, because we are caught up in a glorious, divine expression of intra-Trinitarian love. It is way beyond us. We are, in a sense, saved not as ends in ourselves, but as a means to an end. We don't deserve to be saved. Hell is not unjust. Hell is *just*; eternal punishment is just. But God is merciful to us, not because of some value which we possess natively but because He so values His Son as to give to Him a redeemed humanity who will adore Him forever for saving them, adding a dimension of adoration and praise that angels can't give. And the Son, having received His bride, will give Himself and His bride back to the Father in a reciprocal act of love.

This understanding of redemption is the antidote to superficial, shallow explanations of salvation.

This doctrine of election is not some philosophical abstraction. It is the heart and soul of all redemption. You are a Christian because the Father chose you, the Father wrote your name down, and the Father drew you—therefore, you came. The Son received you, the Son will not lose you, and the Son will raise you on the last day. Finally, the

Father will glorify you because that's what He determined to do before time began. You are precious because of what you have been chosen to do throughout all eternity (cf. Eph 2:7).

When you think about the doctrine of election from that viewpoint, it is just staggering. The Father makes the Son to be sin, in order to pay the price for an unworthy bride (2 Cor 5:21). We, that redeemed bride, were bought by the impoverishing of the Son unto His own death. We are precious now because we have been selected by the Father for the Son.

THINKING BIBLICALLY ABOUT ELECTION

Returning to where we began, I understand that the doctrine of election causes no small controversy. Yet no matter how much fallen human reason and preference might rage against it, this doctrine is inescapably taught throughout Scripture. Therefore, we must bow our knees to this great truth. Once we do that, it becomes the most precious of all doctrines to us.

In closing, let's look at how you ought to think about the doctrine of election. We've just established the first thing we should remember about election: It is pride-crushing. It produces nothing but humility. You don't believe because you were smarter, better, or wiser than anyone else. You believe because you were chosen by God. This is why Spurgeon said, "I know nothing, nothing, again, that is more humbling for us than this doctrine of election."[14] He adds, "I have sometimes fallen prostrate before it, when endeavoring to understand it ... but, when I came near it, and the one thought possessed me—'God hath from the beginning chosen you unto salvation'— ... I was staggered with the mighty thought; and from the dizzy elevation down came my soul, prostrate and broken, saying, 'Lord, I am nothing, I am less than nothing. Why me? Why me?'"[15] That crushing of all pride is at the very heart of worship.

A second thing to remember is that election is God-exalting. It gives God all the glory. This doctrine declares that your ability to understand and believe the truth, to repent from sin, and to submit in faith all comes from God alone. As the psalmist wrote, "Not to us, O Lord, not to us, but to Your name give glory" (Ps 115:1). That is the natural response to the doctrine of election.

Thirdly, I think this doctrine is joy-producing. It plants in your heart overwhelming joy. The mystery of it contributes to the joy; it is the very hopelessness of our own abilities that strengthens that joy. Personally, I continue to be amazed with joy as I meditate on this doctrine.

Psalm 65:4 says, "How blessed is the one whom You choose and bring near to You." If the Lord hadn't chosen us, we'd be like Sodom—destroyed. Rather than question this doctrine, we ought to celebrate it. You have been loved by God with an everlasting love even though you didn't deserve it. Doesn't that produce joy in your heart?

Fourthly, election is a privilege-granting truth. It grants us unspeakable benefits we could never earn. We have been blessed with "every spiritual blessing in the heavenly places in Christ, just as He chose us in Him before the foundation of the world" (Eph 1:3–4). These blessings are ours *solely* because the Father chose us as a gift for the Son.

Fifthly, it is a holiness-producing doctrine. I cannot think of anything more motivating toward a godly life than gratitude for this holy calling. Understanding the doctrine of election produces the most significant impetus for holy living. Again, Spurgeon said, "Nothing.... Nothing under the gracious influence of the Holy Spirit can make a Christian more holy, than the thought that he is chosen. 'Shall I sin ... after God hath chosen me? Shall I transgress [against] such love? Shall I go astray [against such] ... mercy? [Shall I spurn such eternal kindness?] Nay, my God; since thou hast chosen me, I will love thee; I will live [for] thee ... I will give myself to thee ... forever.'"[16]

Sixth and lastly, election is strength-giving. Knowing that I am chosen by God imparts peace in every situation. Philippians 1:6 says, "He who began a good work in you will perfect it until the day of Christ Jesus." If the Father draws you and the Son receives you, He will never lose you. Therein is great encouragement and hope, no matter the circumstances of life. There is a certain boldness and confidence that belong to those who understand that they are chosen and that the gifts and callings of God are irrevocable (Rom 11:29).

What incomparable blessedness attends this doctrine: It crushes pride, exalts God, produces joy, grants unmatched privilege, promotes holiness, and gives great strength.

Dare we ignore such a doctrine? To ignore it or reject it is to steal glory from God. We must glorify God as our redeemer. We must glorify Him as the giver of understanding, repentance, and faith—none of which we can come by on our own. If we deny this doctrine, then we are left misunderstanding our own weakness, and we miss the entire plan of all redemptive history.

Instead, we should echo the words of the apostle Paul in Romans 11:33–36.

> Oh, the depth of the riches both of the wisdom and knowledge of God! How unsearchable are His judgments and unfathomable His ways! For who has known the mind of the Lord, or who became His counselor? Or who has first given to Him that it might be paid back to him again? For from Him and through Him and to Him are all things. To Him be the glory forever. Amen.

ACTUAL ATONEMENT

"I HAD RATHER BELIEVE A LIMITED ATONEMENT THAT IS EFFICACIOUS FOR ALL MEN FOR WHOM IT WAS INTENDED, THAN AN UNIVERSAL ATONEMENT THAT IS NOT EFFICACIOUS FOR ANYBODY, EXCEPT THE WILL OF MAN BE JOINED WITH IT."

CHARLES SPURGEON[17]

A MYSTERY REVEALED

Every doctrine is, in some ways, like an unfinished symphony.

Every major truth of Scripture ends in an unresolved chord because we, with our finite minds, cannot fully grasp the infinity of God's mind. But we work to understand the truth as best we can and leave to Him what is beyond us; in the end, we entrust to Him what we do not understand and embrace with all our hearts what we do. "The secret things belong to the Lord our God, but the things revealed belong to us and to our sons forever, that we may observe all the words of this law" (Deut 29:29).

Certainly, the doctrine of the extent of the atonement is one that takes us far beyond our comfort zone. It stretches our minds to the breaking point. It takes our theology to the perimeter of our tolerances. In the end, it leaves us with some incomprehensible realities—and that's as it should be. Since we are finite and God is infinite, there should be a vast distinction between what we can know and what only He knows. Yet we ought to go to the edge of our comprehension and search the fullness of biblical revelation to understand the greatness and the glory of the work of redemption.

In this chapter I want to answer the crucial question, *For whom did Christ die?* To do this, I'm going to explain the doctrine of *actual atonement*, a more accurate term than the potentially misleading but more widely used *limited atonement*—we will take a closer look at that distinction later on.

For now, it is important to understand that this doctrine—along with the others covered in these chapters—is at the very heart and soul of biblical theology. They are the same doctrines that the Reformation reclaimed from the darkness of Roman Catholicism. They have been expounded by theologians like John Owen[18] and preached by pastors like Charles Spurgeon. And because the doctrine of the atonement is foundational to the gospel, we must understand it correctly.

FOR WHOM DID CHRIST DIE?

For whom did Christ die? The answer may seem obvious to most Christians, but this is often because the topic is considered superficially. And when deep truths such as the atonement receive shallow treatment, the result is that the glorious truth of the matter is lost.

To understand this profound doctrine, let's begin in a simple way. The average Christian today will say that Christ died for everyone. Most Christians believe that Jesus paid for everyone's sin because He loves everyone and wants everyone to be saved. That is the predominant evangelical view. So all we have to do, they will say, is tell sinners that God loves them so much that He paid their penalty and He wants them to be saved—and all they have to do is respond to receive those benefits.

If He died for everyone, then Jesus accomplished only a *potential* salvation on the cross, not an *actual* salvation. That is, sinners have all had their sins atoned for potentially, but that atonement is not actual. They activate it by their faith. So we need to tell sinners to pick up the salvation that's already been purchased for them. Since Christ died for everyone, all can be saved. It's just a matter of coming to receive that salvation. So our responsibility is to convince people to come and accept the gift of salvation that's been provided for them.

This is so enmeshed in the fabric of evangelical theology that many churches assume anyone on the planet can be won to Christ—you just need to figure out the technique for getting unbelievers to a certain psycho-emotive state, and then they'll believe. After all, these evangelicals say, Christ has died for all of them.

The logical fallout of this belief would be *that all the souls in hell are people for whom Christ died*. To put it another way, hell is full of people whose sins were paid for in full on the cross.

Another way to say it would be that the lake of fire, which burns forever with fire and brimstone (Rev 14:10–11; cf. 20:15), is filled with eternally damned people whose offenses against God were completely atoned for by Christ's sacrifice. But that raises the question: Was God's wrath satisfied by Christ's atonement on behalf of those people who will forever stay in hell?

We know that heaven will be populated by the souls of those for whom Christ died. So if Christ died for everyone, He did exactly the same thing for the occupants of hell as He did for the occupants of heaven. The only difference is that the people in heaven accepted the gift, while the people in hell rejected it. That is what the common view boils down to. But it sounds strange when you start to pick it apart, doesn't it?

If Jesus provided the same divine propitiation for the occupants of hell that He did for the occupants of heaven, and the only difference hinges on the sinner's choice, then the death of Jesus Christ is not an actual atonement—it is only a potential atonement. He did not really purchase salvation for anyone in particular; He merely removed a barrier to make it possible for sinners to choose salvation.

So the typical evangelical message to sinners is, "God loves you so much He sent His Son to pay in full the penalty for your sins. Won't you respond to that love and let Him save you, since He has already made atonement for you?" In this system, the decision to activate is up to the sinner.

This message usually carries the notion that God loves you so much because you're special, so He gave His Son to die in your place. That's supposed to move the sinner, emotionally, to love God back and accept His gift. This message is meant to manipulate lost sinners into reaching a certain psychological point—a felt-need point. The goal is to grease the slides and get the sinner moving in the direction of choosing Christ. But this approach has a massive problem: Its very foundation is rotten.

THE PROBLEM OF INABILITY

As we saw in the first chapter, on the doctrine of absolute inability, no sinner can choose salvation by his own wisdom and strength. All are sinners, and all sinners are dead in their trespasses and sins (Eph 2:1). All of them are alienated from the life of God (4:18). They only do evil continually (Gen 6:5). They are unwilling and unable to understand, repent, and believe (1 Cor 2:14). They are blinded by sin and Satan (2 Cor 4:4). They all have hearts that are desperately wicked (Jer 17:9). They all desire only the will of their father, who is Satan (John 8:44). They are all unable to seek God (Rom 3:11). They are all trapped in absolute inability—*unable and unwilling* to do good.

How, then, can any sinner make the choice to activate Christ's atonement? It doesn't matter what felt needs a sinner may have. It doesn't matter how much mood music you play to induce an emotional response—the sinner on his own cannot come to life, cannot repent, and cannot believe.

Remember John 1:12–13, "But as many as received Him, to them He gave the right to become children of God, even to those who believe in His name, who were born, not of blood nor of the will of the flesh nor of the will of man, but of God." And Ephesians 2:8, "For by grace you have been saved through faith; and that not of yourselves, it is the gift of God."

Salvation is from God alone. He has to give life to the dead. He has to give sight to the blind. He has to give hearing to the deaf. He has to give understanding to the ignorant. He has to give repentance to those who love sin. He has to give faith to those who can't believe. He has to move the heart to seek Him that otherwise would not. All the elements that cause the sinner to come to Christ are God-ordained and God-induced.

As we have learned, the doctrine of absolute inability means that *people will only be saved if God saves them*. Therefore, salvation is based upon the decree of God, the sovereign doctrine of election (Eph 1:5). You cannot expect the sinner on his own to choose Christ—no matter how he's emotionally or otherwise prodded. Those who will come to Christ are those whom the Father draws. They are those whom the Father gives to the Son *because He has eternally chosen to do so* (John 6:44, 65; 17:9).

With those truths in mind—the doctrines of absolute inability and divine election—we can ask the question again: For whom did

Christ die? Did He die a death that is a potential salvation for everyone, and therefore in the largest part was fruitless and useless? Or did He die a death that is an actual atonement, accomplishing the salvation of those whom the Father gave to Him in election?

The answer is that Jesus Christ died and paid the *full* penalty for the sins of *all who would ever believe in Him*. His atonement is an actual atonement. He did not provide a potential atonement that can be ignored or disregarded. If Jesus endured the punishment for your sins in its entirety, you're not going to go to hell—that would be a gross miscarriage of justice.

IS THE ATONEMENT LIMITED?

At this point, you may be thinking that I am simply describing limited atonement. And as you are well aware, just mentioning those words raises alarms in many people's minds because we're all so used to hearing that Jesus died for everyone. But as we've just seen, that notion is fraught with obvious problems.

The reality is that I do believe the atonement is limited—and so do you. If you believed the atonement were *un*limited, then you would be a universalist. That is, you would believe that everyone goes to heaven; no one goes to hell. That is the consistent conclusion if you believe that Jesus actually paid the penalty for all the sins of all the people who have ever lived: You have to be a universalist. But to be a universalist, you have to ignore Scripture.

First of all, *atonement* means the sacrifice of Christ by which He paid the penalty for sin and reconciled sinners to God. And we know the atonement is limited because we *know* not everyone is going to heaven; most will end up in hell. Let's begin by looking at some obvious passages. Matthew 10:28 says, "Do not fear those who kill the body but are unable to kill the soul; but rather fear Him who is able to destroy both soul and body in hell." Jesus says the same thing in Luke 12:5. There is a hell, and God is going to send people there. That tells us that the atonement must be limited.

In Mark 9:43, Jesus says, "If your hand causes you to stumble, cut it off; it is better for you to enter life crippled, than, having your two hands, to go into hell, into the unquenchable fire." Again, the reality that hell is prepared for certain people is inescapable. Jesus continues this point in verses 44–48.

In John 8:24 Jesus says, "Therefore I said to you that you will die in your sins; for unless you believe that I am He, you will die in your sins." There is a hell, and people are going there. In fact, Jesus says "many" are going there (Matt 7:13, 22). And the only way to avoid going there—to avoid dying in your sins—is to believe in the Lord Jesus Christ.

How could you "die in your sins" if your sins have been paid for by Christ on the cross? Jesus is clear that the sins of unbelievers are not paid—that they will endure the full penalty for their sins because they died without believing in Him.

In John 3:17–18, Jesus says, "For God did not send the Son into the world to judge the world, but that the world might be saved through Him. He who believes in Him is not judged; he who does not believe has been judged already, because he has not believed in the name of the only begotten Son of God." Every person who does not believe in Christ is judged. Their sins are not atoned for by Christ, so they face the penalty for their wickedness.

Matthew 22:13 agrees: "Then the king said to the servants, 'Bind him hand and foot, and throw him into the outer darkness; in that place there will be weeping and gnashing of teeth'" (cf. 25:30). This is a description of the horrific punishment and judgment that comes upon all who do not receive Christ.

In 2 Thessalonians 1:7–9, Paul repeats the fact that unrepentant sinners are judged for their own sins. He says that the Lord will come "with His mighty angels in flaming fire, dealing out retribution to those who do not know God and to those who do not obey the gospel of our Lord Jesus. These will pay the penalty of eternal destruction, away from the presence of the Lord and from the glory of His power."

The Bible promises there is a hell. It promises that there is punishment for sin. And the only way to avoid it is to not die in your sins. To not die in your sins, you have to believe in the Lord Jesus Christ. If you don't, you're going to pay the penalty of eternal destruction. That punishment proves that the atonement is limited.

We all have to accept the reality of a limited atonement, or else be universalists. We know that not everyone is going to heaven. In fact, it is only few who actually make it there (Matt 7:14). So if we hold on to the idea that Jesus died for everyone, then the vast majority of people for whom Christ died are going to hell. That's very difficult to believe while simultaneously upholding the dignity and perfection of Christ's saving work. So we do believe in a limited atonement—it is limited to those who believe.

HOW IS THE ATONEMENT LIMITED?

Having established that the atonement is limited because not everyone is saved, this leads to an important question: By whom is the atonement limited? What do we mean by calling the atonement "limited"? In what respect is it limited?

To answer that question correctly, we must first look at *who* limits the atonement.

We've just seen the popular view, which would say the atonement itself is unlimited, but that *sinners* limit its *application*, so the atonement is merely potential, and the actuality of it is determined by the sinner. We have to believe, then, that God has provided a sacrifice for sins in His Son that, in and of itself, is not sufficient to atone. It is not inherently effectual because the sinner can neutralize it by rejecting the gospel. So in this view, the sinner is the limiter of the atonement—but there is nothing in Scripture to suggest this is the truth.

On the contrary, Scripture is perfectly clear that God is the one who limits the atonement. And this is the key: He limits it in its *extent*.

We must believe this because God clearly did not choose everyone for salvation, and not everyone will go to heaven. That means you have to accept the fact that God's eternal purpose and decree was never to save everyone.

So the atonement is limited, and it is limited to those who believe, who are those to whom God grants faith (Eph 2:8; Phil 1:29). Thus, the atonement is limited because God limited its extent.

I'm much more comfortable believing that than thinking that sinners can limit the atonement and that Christ's provision of that atonement is therefore wasted on the vast majority of people. If you believe that God provided an atonement which is merely potential, you necessarily believe that He not only limited the atonement's extent but also its *effect*. In other words, if you believe in an unlimited atonement—that Jesus died for everyone—you believe that it is limited in its saving ability. It covers everybody, but not savingly, not efficaciously.

You're likely familiar with the hymn "Jesus Paid It All." Did He "pay it all" *potentially* or *actually*? Did He *actually* bear in His body your sins on the cross or just *potentially* do so? If you want to say that the extent of the atonement is *unlimited*, then you must also say that its *effect* is *limited*, in that it does not apply to anyone in particular. However, the testimony of God's Word is that for those to whom the atonement extends, it has no limits in its efficacy. *Christ actually saves all for whom He died*. J. I. Packer powerfully describes this reality.

> God's saving purpose in the death of his Son was [not] a mere ineffectual wish, depending for its fulfillment on man's willingness to believe, so that for all God could do Christ might have died and none been saved at all.... Christ did not win a hypothetical salvation for hypothetical believers, a mere possibility of salvation for any who might possibly believe, but a real salvation for his own chosen people. His precious blood really does "save us all"; the intended effects of his self-offering do in fact follow, just because the cross was what it was. Its saving power does not depend on faith being added to it; its saving power is such that faith flows from it. The cross secured the full salvation of all for whom Christ died.[19]

So I believe in an atonement limited as to its extent. It is limited to those who believe, those who are chosen by God. But I also believe it is unlimited as to its effect. For those to whom it is secured, it is a full atonement. Jesus did pay it all—actually and powerfully.

The Bible is abundantly clear on these points, as we will see. The hymnwriter got it right. What Christ did on the cross was not a partial, potential, or virtual atonement. It was a real, actual atonement that actually paid for the sins of the elect.

There is no such thing as an atonement by Jesus Christ on the cross that is less than an actual atonement. It is impossible for Jesus to fully pay for your sins on the cross and then require that you pay for them again in hell. That diminishes the work of Christ. To put it bluntly, it *mocks* the work of Christ.

It is unacceptable to believe that hell is full of millions of people whose sins were fully paid for by Christ's sacrifice on the cross. It's repugnant to think that the Father would fully punish the Son on the cross for the sins of people whom He will then again punish for those same sins forever in hell. What Christ did on the cross was a true, full, and complete atonement for the sins of all who will believe. And because no one can believe unless God grants them faith, it is only the sins of those whom the Father has chosen that are paid in full by Christ's atonement. The atonement of Jesus Christ on the cross must be in perfect harmony with the eternal decree of God's election.

It is not biblical to limit the atonement by making it potential and not actual. It is not biblical to limit the atonement by the will of the unwilling and unable sinner. The atonement is limited by God alone, to the elect. But it is unlimited as to its effect. For them, it is a full and complete atonement. If Christ paid the full penalty for your sins, you *will* receive that salvation.

ACTUAL ATONEMENT IN HISTORY

Reformed theologians have consistently taught that the atonement is inherently powerful. Charles Spurgeon explained the difference between actual atonement and the atonement according to Arminians.

> The Arminians say, Christ died for all men. Ask them what they mean by it. Did Christ die so as to secure the salvation of all men? They say, "No, certainly not." We ask them the next question—Did Christ die so as to secure the salvation of any man in particular? They answer, "No." They are obliged to admit this, if they are consistent. They say, "No; Christ has died that any man may be saved if"—and then follow certain conditions of salvation. We say, then, we will just go back to the old statement—Christ did not die so as beyond a doubt to secure the salvation of anybody, did he? You must say "No;" you are obliged to say so.... Now, who is it that limits the death of Christ? Why, you. You say that Christ did not die so as to infallibly secure the salvation of anybody[.] We beg your pardon, when you say we limit Christ's death; we say, "No, my dear sir, it is you that do it.["] We say Christ so died that he infallibly secured the salvation of a multitude that no man can number, who through Christ's death not only may be saved, but are saved, must be saved, and cannot by any possibility run the hazard of being anything but saved. You are welcome to your

atonement; you may keep it. We will never renounce ours for the sake of it.[20]

Spurgeon understood that the atonement is an actual atonement, not a potential one. It is a real atonement, not simply a barrier removed. But the reason this wonderful doctrine is found throughout history is not due to the genius of men like Spurgeon. It is found throughout the history of the church because *it is taught in Scripture*. That is where the truly rich explanation of this doctrine lies—and there is where we will look next.

ACTUAL ATONEMENT IN CHRIST'S PURPOSE

I intend to take you into the depths of what Scripture has to say, to show you why we are so adamant in upholding this marvelous view of the atonement. Let's begin by looking at Christ's goal in the incarnation. Jesus came into the world, as He said, "to seek and to save that which was lost" (Luke 19:10). He came into this world to *rescue* sinners, not to potentially rescue sinners.

Paul wrote something similar to Timothy: "It is a trustworthy statement, deserving full acceptance, that Christ Jesus came into the world to save sinners, among whom I am foremost of all" (1 Tim 1:15). Five times in the pastoral epistles, Paul uses the little phrase "It is a trustworthy statement" (1 Tim 1:15; 3:1; 4:9; 2 Tim 2:11; Titus 3:8). There's little doubt what it means. It indicates a recognized saying that had already developed in the early church. It isn't something Paul is saying for the first time, but something he is quoting that he knew everyone understood as a trustworthy saying.

It seems that by the time Paul wrote 1 Timothy, which was after his first imprisonment, a fairly well-articulated theology had already developed. There were some creeds, hymns, and faithful sayings which were recognized by the church. They are summaries of key doctrines which should be believed and approved by all Christians. Thus, the summary phrase in 1 Timothy 1:15 was no doubt a familiar statement to Timothy's church, as well as to Timothy himself.

The saying "Christ Jesus came into the world to save sinners" acts as a condensed articulation of the gospel. Every word was chosen carefully. The church had summarized the gospel in this one brief statement. The very purpose that Christ had in the incarnation was the redemption of sinners—not a potential redemption of sinners.

The coming of the Lord Jesus was the perfect revelation of God. God's character, purpose, and will were all seen in Jesus because He is God. So we conclude that God is by nature a Savior because He came into the world to seek and save that which was lost. This is why the apostle Paul loves to call Him "God our Savior" (1 Tim 1:1; 2:3; Titus 1:3). But in order for God to save sinners, there had to be a sacrifice that paid the penalty for their sins.

Second Corinthians 5:21 says God made Christ "to be sin on our behalf." That is an actual atonement, as the Lord was punished by the Father for the sins of His people.

ACTUAL ATONEMENT IN CHRIST'S SACRIFICE

The Son of God came into the world as a man to offer Himself as a sacrifice—an unimaginable condescension. On the cross Jesus died not merely under the wrath of men, but under the wrath of God. He was put to death not only by the actions of the Romans and the Jews, but by the predetermined plan of God (Acts 2:23). So He bore the wrath of God for all the sinners who would ever believe in Him. While it was a substitutionary sacrifice for Christ to do this, it was also a satisfying sacrifice. It was the very purpose He came to fulfill—to save His people by satisfying the wrath of God for them.

To understand the sacrifice of Christ, there is no better place to start than Isaiah 53. This is the classic Old Testament passage which deals with the substitutionary death of the Messiah. Isaiah is inspired to write of Messiah's death in verse 4, "Surely our griefs He Himself bore, and our sorrows He carried; yet we ourselves esteemed Him stricken, smitten of God, and afflicted."

The Hebrew word for "griefs" is "sickness." It's a broad term that can refer to diseases, infirmities, and calamities. Here, sins are viewed from the perspective of what they produce. A life of sin becomes full of sickness, disease, infirmity, and calamity. These are the griefs Isaiah writes about. Christ "bore" these on our behalf by suffering for sin on the cross, the word "bore" simply meaning to lift up, pick up, and place on oneself. Christ dealt with all the effects of sin by taking sin upon Himself.

Then Isaiah writes it another way: "Our sorrows He carried." "Sorrows" is a word for pains. "Griefs" refers to the outward effects of sin, but "sorrows" refers mostly to the inward effect of sin. Sin is viewed here not as a moral entity, as the word "sin" usually conveys, but rather again from a perspective of consequences—from the distress and horrors of life that flow out of sin.

So Christ picked up sin, with all that it produces, and put it on Himself. He carried it to the cross, and He bore the full punishment of God's wrath. "The LORD was pleased to crush Him," Isaiah writes in verse 10. Messiah took the punishment for our sin and thus carried the full weight of sin and all its effects away.

Verses 5 and 6 continue this idea. "He was pierced through for our transgressions, He was crushed for our iniquities; the chastening for our well-being fell upon Him, and by His scourging we are healed. All of us like sheep have gone astray, each of us has turned to his own way; but the LORD has caused the iniquity of us all to fall on Him."

This passage is not saying Jesus sympathetically felt our pain. He actually took upon Himself our sin and its punishment, paid for it in full, and thus put an end in our lives to the reign of sin with all of its effects. We have been freed from sin's penalty and power, and one day when we enter heaven, we will also be freed from sin's presence.

We should have suffered for our sins, but He did instead. He took away all the judgment we deserved—even eternal punishment—and put it on Himself. Thus He shifted the load completely away from us. This concept of a substitutionary sacrifice is consistent throughout the Old Testament.

On the Day of Atonement, described in Leviticus 16, when the atonement was made, one animal was killed and one animal was kept alive (Lev 16:7–10). The priest would lay his hands on the live animal, designated the scapegoat, symbolically placing all the sins of the people on that scapegoat, which he would send out into the wilderness, never to return again (vv. 20–22). Jesus atones for the sins of believers in the same way—He is the scapegoat. He picks up all the sin that belongs on us and carries it Himself.

Did Jesus do this actually or potentially? The Savior in Isaiah 53 is described as actually bearing sin, not potentially bearing sin. We know this because Isaiah 53:10, speaking of the Messiah, says, "He will see His offspring, He will prolong His days." The passage shifts into future tense to show the results of what the Messiah has done. He will see His posterity—all the ones He brings to salvation.

That message reminds us of Jesus' words in John 6:37–39: "All that the Father gives Me will come to Me, and the one who comes to Me I will certainly not cast out. For I have come down from heaven, not to do My own will, but the will of Him who sent Me. This is the will of Him who sent Me, that of all that He has given Me I lose nothing, but raise it up on the last day."

Not only will He live to see His posterity, but as Isaiah 53:11 says, He will be satisfied when He sees this accomplishment of salvation fully realized.

But who are the Messiah's posterity? Verse 12 answers, "He Himself bore the sin of *many*" (emphasis added). The "many" (notice: not "the all") refers to those who believe, the elect of God. Those people—and those alone—are the ones for whose sins He died and atoned. Those are the ones He will justify. As verse 11 says, "The Righteous One, My Servant, will justify the *many*" (emphasis added). By actually taking on their sins, He would take the punishment they deserved. This view from Isaiah 53 paints the picture of the substitutionary sacrifice of the Messiah who effectually bears the sins of His posterity, not a Messiah who potentially bears the sins of every person whether they believe or not.

ACTUAL ATONEMENT AND EVANGELISM

As we saw earlier, Paul tells us in 1 Timothy 1:15 that the Lord Jesus came into the world to save sinners. That's the great enterprise. God is a Savior. Christ then, as God manifest in the flesh, does a saving work. And all those that He saves are mandated to proclaim this work. According to the Great Commission, we are to make disciples of all nations (Matt 28:19). We are ambassadors for Christ, begging people to be reconciled to God (2 Cor 5:20). We have been redeemed for this great evangelistic enterprise.

In Acts 1:8, as Jesus leaves this world, His final words to His disciples institute the church's evangelistic work: "You will receive power when the Holy Spirit has come upon you; and you shall be My witnesses both in Jerusalem, and in all Judea and Samaria, and even to the remotest part of the earth." That's the last thing Jesus said on earth. He instructed His followers to pick up the glorious gospel of salvation and take it to the ends of the earth.

That's why we, the individual members of the church, are here. Everything else is secondary. I never want to diminish that fact. There is no inconsistency in teaching the doctrines of absolute inability, divine election, and actual atonement while also emphasizing evangelism. Evangelism is our mandate; it is believers' reason for being on earth.

We will worship far better in heaven. We will serve the Lord far better in heaven. We will love each other far better in heaven. In fact, we will do all of that perfectly in heaven. But one thing we will *not* do in heaven is evangelize the lost. They won't be there. So God, who weeps over the lost through the eyes of Jeremiah (Jer 13:17), and Jesus, who Himself wept over the lost in Jerusalem (Luke 19:41; cf. 13:34), call on us to weep over the impenitent and to go forth bearing precious truth with tears.

That evangelistic mandate defines why the church is in the world. We are told to pray for the salvation of all people (1 Tim 2:1–2). We are told to set a godly example and to live our lives as shining lights so that men might glorify God (Matt 5:14–16). We are told to proclaim the gospel to Jews and Gentiles alike without being ashamed of it (Rom 1:16). And the offer of the gospel is a legitimate offer.

Every sinner on the planet is accountable for the response he gives to God's truth. Every man has a stewardship that God has given him. It may be the stewardship of a law written in his heart (Rom 2:14–16) or the stewardship of his rational mind, which sees creation and concludes that God made it all (1:18–20). But we know this: Not everybody will repent, and not everybody will believe.

There are innumerable souls even now that have left this earth and are facing eternal torment. That fact is inescapable. There is an eternal hell, and it will be continually filled with sinners until redemptive history is over—sinners who ignored the truth of God however it was presented to them. And if, while in hell, they were to be given the opportunity to choose differently, they wouldn't. They showed no interest in God then, and they have no interest in Him now.

Sinners are accountable for how they respond to the message at whatever level they receive it. But if we know that thousands of people will reject the truth of the gospel and end up in hell, why do we still preach to them? To answer this, we can look back at Isaiah 6.

This chapter contains God's calling of the prophet Isaiah. In verse 8, the Lord asks, "Whom shall I send, and who will go for Us?" The people of God are in serious trouble. The previous chapter lays out their characteristic sins and the severe judgment that was coming. So God was sending a messenger to call the people to repentance before the judgment came.

Isaiah responds, "Here am I. Send me!" (v. 8). This, of course, should be every believer's response. Then the Lord replies with a bizarre statement, "Go, and tell this people: 'Keep on listening, but do not perceive; keep on looking, but do not understand.' Render the hearts of this people insensitive, their ears dull, and their eyes dim, otherwise they might see with their eyes, hear with their ears, understand with their hearts, and return and be healed" (vv. 9–10).

God is saying that Israel is going to hear but not understand. They're going to see but not comprehend. They're going to be insensitive, dull of hearing, and dim of sight. They won't repent, so they won't be healed.

Isaiah asks the logical follow-up question in verse 11, "Lord, how long?" He wants to know how long he has to preach to an audience that will reject the truth—you can sympathize with Isaiah here. God responds that the prophet is to keep at it "until cities are devastated and without inhabitant, houses are without people and the land is utterly desolate, the Lord has removed men far away, and the forsaken places are many in the midst of the land" (vv. 11–12). Isaiah was commanded to preach until Israel was desolate and no one was left to listen to him.

This may seem fruitless, but verse 13 is the key, "Yet there will be a tenth portion in it." The Lord says there will be a remnant—a tenth of Israel. Verse 13 concludes by calling the remnant "the holy seed." This group was chosen by the Lord for salvation.

This is the same "seed," the same offspring, that the Messiah saw in Isaiah 53:10. It is no mystery to God who will be saved. He is the one who told us that it will be few (Matt 7:14). The word "holy" (Isa 6:13) means "set apart." Those who will be saved are those who have already been set apart by God.

So we go like Isaiah went. We go to the world with the gospel, knowing that most people will not believe. We could be very discouraged by such a task, but we can be assured that the Lord has set aside a remnant for salvation. These people are already set apart by God for His own purposes (Eph 1:11). They are the elect, so they will, upon hearing the gospel, repent and believe.

We see this in Acts 13:48, "When the Gentiles heard this, they began rejoicing and glorifying the word of the Lord; and as many as had been appointed to eternal life believed." Those who had been "*appointed to eternal life*" are the ones who believed. That means not everyone—just the remnant, the holy seed.

In Acts 18:9–10, the Lord came to Paul in a vision saying, "Do not be afraid any longer, but go on speaking and do not be silent; for I am with you, and no man will attack you in order to harm you, for I have many people in this city." Those people weren't converted yet, but they were God's. Paul was instructed to preach the gospel because God already had His holy seed there. They were just waiting to hear the gospel.

So who will be saved at the preaching of the gospel? We've seen from Scripture that no sinner on his own can or will seek God. His condition of being dead in sin makes that impossible (Eph 2:1). So the only ones who can come are those to whom God gives life, and God gives life only to those whom He has chosen (John 3:4–8; Eph 1:5). God chooses whom He will save, and God saves whom He has chosen.

In this way, salvation is all of God. God saves His holy seed, in the language of Isaiah 6. And the Messiah atones for the sins of His offspring, in the language of Isaiah 53. God's election and actual atonement guarantee the success of evangelism. Far from hindering evangelism, the doctrine of actual atonement gives the evangelist the certainty that God will save the people He has chosen through the preaching of the gospel.

Yet even with this knowledge, some people still raise objections against this glorious doctrine.

DIDN'T CHRIST DIE FOR THE WORLD?

At this point, many object to the doctrine of actual atonement by pointing to those passages that say Christ died for the "world." So let's look at Scripture to see how we should understand that term; let's survey the New Testament to see how it is used there.

When we hear the word *world*, we might think it refers to every person in existence. But that's not always the biblical use of the term. John writes in John 1:9, "There was the true Light which, coming into the world, enlightens every man." Does that mean He came to every human being on the face of the earth? No, it just means He came into the human realm. "Coming into the world" refers not to every living person but to a place.

John continues in verse 10, "He was in the world, and the world was made through Him." "World" is just a term for creation here. He was in the world as God incarnate. It is clearly not a reference to every single individual on the planet. So the word *world* has to be qualified and interpreted in context.

We see this again in John 1:29, "Behold, the Lamb of God who takes away the sin of the world!" We have to qualify that immediately. If He took away the sin of every person on earth, everybody would be saved. So we have to qualify the word "world" here. But how?

As we saw in John 1:9–10, God the Son came into the human realm to take away sin. Then, in verse 11, John tells us, "He came to His own, and those who were His own did not receive Him." Then he adds in verse 12, "But as many as received Him, to them He gave the right to become children of God, even to those who believe in His name." So taking away the sin of the world is qualified to apply only to whoever believed in Him. They alone have the right to be forgiven and become children of God. So *world* is just a generic term meaning the created order, and it has to be qualified properly.

In John 3:16–17, perhaps the most famous instance of *world* in Scripture, Jesus says, "For God so loved the world, that He gave His only begotten Son, that whoever believes in Him shall not perish, but have eternal life. For God did not send the Son into the world to judge the world, but that the world might be saved through Him." Immediately, we know if we don't qualify "world" here, that makes us universalists, and we know that's wrong because the Bible is clear that there is eternal punishment. So we must qualify "world" here, and it's clear that it refers to humanity or humankind. These verses don't teach that God is going to save every individual person; they simply teach God's love for humanity.

He loved people from all tribes and tongues and nations. But His saving love for the world is limited to those within the world—that is, the human realm of creation—*who believe*. "God so loved the world, that He gave His only begotten Son, that *whoever believes in* Him shall not perish" (John 3:16, emphasis added).

John 4:42 says the same thing: "It is no longer because of what you said that we believe, for we have heard for ourselves and know that this One is indeed the Savior of the world." It doesn't say Christ might be or could be Savior of the world; He "*is indeed* the Savior of the world."

He is Savior in an absolute, unqualified sense. Therefore, we must conclude that "world" has to be qualified because if you try to protect a universal understanding of "world" in this passage, you necessarily end up limiting "Savior." That is, you will limit either the effect of Christ's saving work, or its extent.

So He is the Savior of the world in this sense: He's the only Savior the human race will ever know. The world has no other Savior. What's really important to remember throughout the gospel of John—whenever you read "the Savior of the world," "God so loved the world," and "He was in the world"—is that John was addressing an environment of Jewish anti-Gentile racism. That the Messiah is for the world, meaning for Jews and Gentiles alike, was a foreign concept. It was a revolutionary perspective for the Jewish reader.

Jesus emphasizes this point again in John 6:33, "The bread of God is that which comes down out of heaven, and gives life to the world." "World" is qualified in verse 35: "I am the bread of life; he who comes to Me will not hunger, and he who believes in Me will never thirst." The Bread of God gives life to the world—both Jews and Gentiles—if they come to Him.

Another of John's writings confirms this reading of *world*. First John 4:14 says, "We have seen and testify that the Father has sent the Son to be the Savior of the world." The point here is likewise that the saving work of Christ is not limited to the Jews but encompasses "the world," which is made up of both Jews and Gentiles.

John 6:33 is followed by verse 51, "I am the living bread that came down out of heaven; if anyone eats of this bread, he will live forever; and the bread also that I will give for the life of the world is My flesh." He gives His life for the "world," but who is the "world"? It says in the same verse, "[Whoever] eats of this bread, he will live forever."

Even though Jesus is the only Savior for the world, that is both Jews and Gentiles, salvation—including the atonement—is always qualified as belonging only unto the believing. We saw this with the Bread of God in John 6:33. It gives life to the "world." But verse 35 limits salvation to those who come to Christ. This is emphasized again in verse 51. Only those who come to Christ and eat the bread live, not every person who ever lived.

We see John 12:47 affirm the same truths in the same language. "If anyone hears My sayings and does not keep them, I do not judge him; for I did not come to judge the world, but to save the world." As we have established, obviously this does not mean that He will save every human being who's ever lived. So "world" must be qualified in some sense, and it simply means that He will extend His salvation without regard for ethnicity, class, or sex across this planet—His salvation will encompass humanity in general. So will His judgment.

Another illustration qualifying the word "world" can be found in John 14:22, "Judas (not Iscariot) said to Him, 'Lord, what then has happened that You are going to disclose Yourself to us and not to the world?'" What do you think Judas meant by that? He certainly didn't mean that Jesus did not disclose Himself to any human being on the planet. "World" here clearly refers to the wider realm of humanity outside the narrow group of the disciples—the general public.

Jesus even provides His own qualifications on the word "world." In John 17:6, Jesus prays for "the men whom You gave Me out of the world." Then in verse 9, He adds, "I ask on their behalf; I do not ask on behalf of the world, but of those whom You have given Me; for they are Yours." Jesus indicates He is not interceding for all of humanity in an unqualified manner, but for the specific people whom God gave Him *out of* it. Jesus Himself makes it clear that He doesn't intend to save every single person who ever lived, only those whom God chose out of the "world."

Continuing in verse 15, as He prays for His own, Jesus says, "I do not ask You to take them out of the world, but to keep them from the evil one." Here He uses the "world" to mean human enterprise with all its sin. In verse 16 He says, "They are not of the world," and in verse 18, "As You sent Me into the world, I also have sent them into the world." But again, verse 9, Jesus does not intercede for the "world"—only for those chosen by the Father. So Jesus also spoke of the "world" in a limited, qualified sense.

In fact, as the Pharisees were growing increasingly troubled about Jesus, John 12:19 records they "said to one another, 'You see that you are not doing any good; look, the world has gone after Him.'" They obviously did not think that every human being that ever lived had gone after Christ. As in every other case, the word "world" must be qualified.

So having examined the contexts, we understand the term *world* as employed simply to get us beyond the narrowness and racism of Judaism. Scripture uses this word to show us that the extent of the atonement stretches across the earth to all times and all nations. Paul in Romans 11:15 says that the rejection of Israel has brought about "the reconciliation of the world." Again, the apostle doesn't believe for a moment that every single person who ever lived will be reconciled to God. He means that because of Israel's rejection, the church is grafted in and is made up of both Jew and Gentile.

The Jews struggled with this truth. In Acts 10, Peter preached the gospel to Cornelius and a group of Gentiles. Verse 44 says, "While Peter was still speaking these words, the Holy Spirit fell upon all those who were listening to the message." The result of this is recorded in verse 45: "All the circumcised believers [converts from Judaism] who came with Peter were amazed, because the gift of the Holy Spirit had been poured out on the Gentiles also." That astonishment was due to the Jews' provincialism. But the gospel was never intended to be limited to Israel. It was for the world.

The same can be seen in Acts 15. At the Council of Jerusalem, Peter stands up and says in verses 7–9, "Brethren, you know that in the early days God made a choice among you, that by my mouth the Gentiles would hear the word of the gospel and believe. And God, who knows the heart, testified to them giving them the Holy Spirit, just as He also did to us; and He made no distinction between us and them, cleansing their hearts by faith." The gospel stretched outside of Judaism to the rest of humanity—to people in every tongue, tribe, people, and nation.

Two more passages deserve our attention, although we'll treat them briefly. First John 2:2 says, "He Himself is the propitiation for our sins; and not for ours only, but also for those of the whole world." What is this verse saying? Once again, the point is that actual propitiation has been made for people from all different ethnicities and nations. This verse makes the same point that John makes over and over again throughout his gospel, the same point that Peter made in the book of Acts and that Paul makes in Romans 11: The gospel is not limited to the Jews.

"Propitiation" (Gk., *hilasmos*) in 1 John 2:2 is a very strong word. It denotes the actual satisfying of God's just wrath. It's not a potential satisfaction. It could be translated "placated" or "satisfied." Christ Himself is the satisfaction. He is the placation. He propitiates God's anger for our sins. But not just ours, as a narrow group of people, but "those of the whole world." Because of that phrasing, some people insist on interpreting this verse as teaching an unlimited atonement. I responded to this view in my commentary on this passage:

> Logically, such an interpretation strips the work of Christ on the cross of any actual atonement for anyone specifically, and it provides only a potential satisfaction for God's wrath....
>
> To be faithful to the truth revealed in Scripture, "the whole world" must be comprehended as a generic expression that refers to humanity throughout the earth, but not necessarily to every individual. "World" simply identifies the earthly realm of mankind to which God directed His reconciling love and

> provided propitiation (cf. John 1:29; 3:16; 6:51; 1 Tim. 2:5–6; Titus 2:11; Heb. 2:9). The language of Scripture is strong and clear, stating that Christ's death actually satisfies fully and eternally the demands of God's wrath for those who believe (John 10:11, 15; 17:9, 20; Acts 20:28; Rom. 8:32, 37; Eph. 5:25). Though the Savior's death intrinsically had infinite value, it was designed to actually (not potentially) secure the satisfaction for divine justice only on behalf of those who would believe.[21]

"Propitiation" is far too strong and clear a word to be understood as communicating mere potential. It always refers to an actual satisfaction. God was satisfied with Messiah's sacrifice on behalf of all believers. On the ultimate Day of Atonement, Jesus was the sacrificial lamb whose blood sprinkled before God was a true satisfaction. Propitiation turned God's wrath away forever—and not just for us, but for everyone who believes.

Finally, in 2 Corinthians 5:19, Paul writes, "God was in Christ reconciling the world to Himself." Paul describes "reconciling" in this verse as "God ... not counting their trespasses against them." If "world" means every single person who ever lived, then what do you do with everybody in hell? If God does not count their trespasses against them, how can He then punish them for those same trespasses in hell? So, as in every other instance of the word, "world" here must be qualified. As we've now established many times over, an unlimited atonement logically results in either double jeopardy or universalism.

Note that Paul says, "God was ... reconciling," not, "God was making reconciliation possible." God did not merely remove a barrier to reconciliation. He did not give nine-tenths and tell the sinner to close the final gap. He definitively reconciled "the world" to Himself through Christ's atoning death. He does not count their trespasses against them because they were counted against Christ. Friend, if He does not count your trespasses against you, that means He bore your transgressions in full. If you believe in Him, you are under no condemnation (Rom 8:1).

That is not a potential salvation; that is an actual salvation. Whoever "the world" is here, they no longer have their trespasses counted against them. Second Corinthians 5:17 tells us "the world" is those who are new creatures in Christ. They are those verse 21 speaks of: "He made Him who knew no sin to be sin on our behalf." Whose behalf? Not everyone who ever lived, but only those who "become the righteousness of God in [Christ]."

So whenever we see the term *world*, we must properly qualify it. There could be no hell for sinners if Christ has paid in full, provided reconciliation, and satisfied God's wrath for every human being in the world. So we know *world* simply indicates no ethnic or national limits.

DIDN'T CHRIST DIE FOR ALL?

We have seen how Scripture uses the word *world* in relation to Christ's atoning work. But what about those passages that use the word *all* in connection with the atonement? Let's look at some of those.

Romans 5:18, "So then as through one transgression there resulted condemnation to all men, even so through one act of righteousness there resulted justification of life to all men." That one transgression was Adam's sin, and it did affect everybody who ever lived. But then Paul adds, "Even so through one act of righteousness there resulted justification of life to all men." If you're not careful here—if you drive the parallel in the wrong direction—you're going to come to the conclusion that every person who ever lived is justified in Christ. But that is obviously not true.

There's only one illustration being made throughout this passage. Paul is talking about the impact of the work of Christ—how the work of Christ redeems all who believe. The question that forms in the reader's mind is, How can one man's act have such a great effect and such massive implications? So Paul makes the parallel.

The apostle simply argues that by one man's sin, everybody who died, died. And by one man's righteousness, everybody who became righteous, became righteous. He even changes his terminology in verse 19—just to make sure we don't think "all" is universal—and says, "As through the one man's disobedience *the many* were made sinners, even so through the obedience of the One *the many* will be made righteous" (emphasis added). He put that in there purposely to back us off the wrong understanding of verse 18, which might tempt us to think everybody is saved. So again, "all" is properly qualified by its context.[22]

We find another "all" in Romans 8:32. Paul writes, "He who did not spare His own Son, but delivered Him over for us all." Who are the "all" here? Some people say Christ was delivered up for everybody in the whole world. But Paul doesn't just say "all," he says "us all." So who is the "us" that Paul refers to?

Just one verse earlier, Romans 8:31 says, "If God is for us, who is against us?" Does "us" here refer to every person who ever lived? Is God "for" everybody in the whole world? No. This is a qualified "us." Verses 29–30 clarify further who the "us" is: "For those whom He foreknew, He also predestined to become conformed to the image of His Son, so that He would be the firstborn among many brethren; and these whom He predestined, He also called; and these whom He called, He also justified; and these whom He justified, He also glorified." The "us" refers to those who were predestined, called, justified, and glorified. To put it another way, verse 33 says, "Who will bring a charge against God's elect?" So it is clear that the elect are the "us all" from verse 32.

One final passage containing "all" is 2 Corinthians 5:14–15. Paul writes in these verses, "For the love of Christ controls us, having concluded this, that one died for all, therefore all died; and He died for all, so that they who live might no longer live for themselves, but for Him who died and rose again on their behalf." If we follow the logic of the verse carefully, this "all," also, must be qualified.

Some people read this verse and conclude that Jesus died for every person that ever lived. But Paul writes, "[He] died for all, therefore all died." What does this mean? When you came to Christ, you died—this is the case for every believer. In Galatians 2:20, Paul testifies, "I have been crucified with Christ." In Romans 6:3–7, Paul teaches that believers have been baptized into Christ's death. In Him you die. This is what Paul is talking about in 2 Corinthians 5:14 when he writes, "[He] died for all, therefore all died." Christ died for the "all" who died in Him.

Verse 15 makes this even clearer: "He died for all ... they who live." He died for those who have died and now live in Him. He "died and arose again on their behalf"—on their behalf actually, not on everyone's behalf potentially. Christ was an efficacious substitute for His people, not an impotent substitute for no one in particular.[23]

DID CHRIST DIE FOR FALSE TEACHERS?

Second Peter 2:1 has caused many to believe that Christ died even for unbelievers. Peter writes, "But false prophets also arose among the people, just as there will also be false teachers among you, who will secretly introduce destructive heresies, even denying the Master who bought them, bringing swift destruction upon themselves."

In what sense did Christ buy these false teachers? There are two ways to view it. First, you can see it as universal provision for the redemption of sinners, even though they refuse it and are damned. In this view, Christ provided an impotent atonement for nobody in particular. So it's clear that we have to understand this in another sense.

The correct way to understand this verse is that these false teachers had identified themselves with Christ's redemption, claiming Him as the One who bought them. They claimed Him as their Redeemer, and their word was taken at face value—even though He never really was their "Master."

The word "Master" here is the Greek word *despotēs*, the clear origin for our English word *despot*. It means lord or ruler in an absolute sense. This term appears ten times in the New Testament, and it always refers to one who has supreme authority. It can denote the master of a house or estate who has full authority over everybody else in it (1 Tim 6:1, 2; Titus 2:9; 1 Pet 2:18), or to God or Christ (Luke 2:29; Acts 4:24; 2 Tim 2:21; Jude 4; Rev 6:10).

It's important to understand that Peter is using sarcasm in 2 Peter 2:1. These false teachers claimed to be true believers and true teachers. These charlatans infiltrated the church, and Peter says to them, "You have denied the Master who, you claim, bought you." Their very lives show that Christ never was their Master; they never truly belonged to Him. I explain this in my commentary on 2 Peter:

> The phrase "who bought them" fits Peter's analogy perfectly. He is alluding to the master of a house who would purchase slaves and put them in charge of various household tasks. Because they were now regarded as the master's personal property, they owed their complete allegiance to him. While false teachers maintain that they are part of Christ's household, they deny such professions through their actions—refusing to become servants under His authority. "Bought" (*agorazō*) means "to purchase," or "to redeem out of the marketplace," and in this context is parallel to Deuteronomy 32:5–6 (cf. Zeph. 1:4–6). The false teachers of Peter's day claimed Christ as their Redeemer, yet they refused to accept His sovereign lordship, thus revealing their true character as unregenerate enemies of biblical truth.[24]

We know the Master didn't pay the price for damnable heretics. Such people profess Him as Master and profess that He died for them, but their profession—like the rest of their teaching—is false.

CHRIST DIED FOR MANY

One way to better understand the extent of Christ's atonement is to look at the word *many* in Scripture—it has a number of interesting usages that shed light on Christ's saving work.

We've already looked at Isaiah 53, but consider again what we're told in verses 11–12: "The Righteous One, My Servant, will justify the many.... He Himself bore the sin of many." Isaiah predicted that the Messiah would offer a vicarious or substitutionary death on behalf of "many." Messiah would justify not all, but "many" by dying as their substitute.

We saw this also in Romans 5:19, which says that the Lord died not for all, but for many. The same idea appears in Hebrews 9:28, "Christ ... [has] been offered once to bear the sins of many." "Many" is simply another way of saying "less than everyone."

Jesus Himself used this terminology in Matthew 20:28, "The Son of Man did not come to be served, but to serve, and to give His life a ransom for many" (cf. Mark 10:45). Who are the many? They are all those who will believe. Christ was an actual ransom, just like He was an actual satisfaction and substitution. He achieved an effectual atonement for all who would believe.

CHRIST DIED FOR HIS PEOPLE

So Scripture teaches that Christ died for "many," but it gets even more specific than that. An angel came to Joseph before Jesus' birth, saying, "Joseph, son of David, do not be afraid to take Mary as your wife; for the Child who has been conceived in her is of the Holy Spirit. She will bear a Son; and you shall call His name Jesus, for He will save His people from their sins" (Matt 1:20–21). He would not save everyone; He would save "*His people*." The Bible never speaks of a potential salvation or a potential atonement. Christ provided a real salvation for His people.

In John 10:11, Jesus states even more explicitly whom He died for. "I am the good shepherd; the good shepherd lays down His life for the sheep." In verses 14–15 He adds, "I am the good shepherd, and I know My own and My own know Me, even as the Father knows Me and I know the Father; and I lay down My life for the sheep." The word "for" here is the Greek preposition *huper*, which means "on behalf of" or "for the benefit of." This word appears in many passages that speak about substitutionary atonement (see Mark 14:24; Luke 22:19–20; John 6:51; Rom 5:6, 8; Gal 3:13; 1 Pet 3:18). The Good Shepherd died not on behalf of every person who ever lived, but on behalf of His sheep, whom He already knows by name (John 10:3, 14–15). There are specific sheep for which Christ actually atoned.

There is a similar statement in John 11:49–52,

> Caiaphas, who was high priest that year, said to them, "You know nothing at all, nor do you take into account that it is expedient for you that one man die for the people, and that the whole nation not perish." Now he did not say this on his own initiative, but being high priest that year, he prophesied that Jesus was going to die for the nation, and not for the nation only, but in order that He might also gather together into one the children of God who are scattered abroad.

What a statement! Jesus died not just for the Jews, but to gather into one body the children of God scattered all over the world. He died for a particular body of people scattered throughout the earth.

Paul also informs our understanding of the extent of the atonement when he writes about marriage. Ephesians 5:25 says, "Husbands, love your wives, just as Christ also loved the church and gave Himself up for her." He paid the price for His bride, the church. He redeemed her. It wasn't a redemption of everyone in general; it was a redemption of His own church, in particular.

It was a particular redemption. God chose the church in Christ before the foundation of the world (Eph 1:4). He predestined us through Christ according to His will (v. 5). It is in Christ alone that we have redemption (v. 7). We are "God's own possession" (v. 14). Therefore, the church is a specific people, redeemed by God for His own possession, those in whose place Christ died (5:25).

Paul makes the same point in Titus 2:13–14. He says believers are "looking for the blessed hope and the appearing of the glory of our great God and Savior, Christ Jesus, who gave Himself for us to redeem us from every lawless deed, and to purify for Himself a people for His own possession." And who was that people? Those whom God chose before the foundation of the world and gave to the Son as His bride. He purchased a specific people as His bride, not an undefined or indefinite throng.

Peter says, "He Himself bore our sins in His body on the cross" (1 Pet 2:24). He died for "*our* sins," that is, the sins of believers. He also says, "Christ also died for sins once for all, the just for the unjust, so that He might bring us to God" (3:18). Christ didn't die so that maybe people might come to God; He died to actually and definitively bring us to God. His death satisfied God as the redemption price for His holy seed, the holy offspring.

CHRIST MADE AN ACTUAL ATONEMENT

The sum of these questions comes down to this: Is the death of Christ a work that potentially saves willing sinners, or is it one that actually saves unwilling sinners made willing by God's sovereign grace? The only possible answer is that God provided a sacrifice in His Son that was a true and complete payment for the sins of all who would ever believe. And all of those will believe because the Father will draw them, and grant them regeneration, repentance, and faith. Jesus' death, then, must be understood as a full satisfaction of God's holy justice on behalf of the elect whom God wills to save.

If the opposite is true, He died for all potentially, and no one actually. The actualizing of the atonement would depend upon the sinner, and if the sinner chose not to receive Christ, then Christ's death for him was no real atonement, but an unrealized potential.

People who hold the latter position like to say they do not believe in a limited atonement, but that's simply untrue. The reality is that they believe in an atonement which is limited in its reality and power. They want to believe that it is unlimited in its extent—that it was accomplished on behalf of everyone without exception. But that severely diminishes its efficacy.

The Bible teaches just the opposite. The atonement is limited in its extent, not its efficacy, encompassing only those whom God chooses and saves. For all of that number, it is unlimited in its effect and power. It is, then, *not a potential salvation for all*; it is *an actual salvation for the many*. And who are the many? They are the holy seed, the offspring, the chosen of the Father, the bride of the Son, and the sheep of the Good Shepherd.

This clarity changes everything.

If you believe that there is a potential atonement floating around the world and you just have to convince sinners to pick it up, then evangelism takes on a completely different complexion. It becomes an exercise in convincing the sinner to actualize the atonement. But who gets the credit for that type of salvation?

In fact, the atonement isn't even enough to save you, in this system. Isn't that shocking? Jesus dying on the cross and paying the penalty for sin isn't enough to redeem anybody in this scheme. *You* have to complete it—which sounds inescapably like salvation by works. But how can the sinner do that when he is absolutely unable and unwilling to do so?

It's repugnant to look at the cross and see Jesus, at the very end of His torment, looking up and saying, "It is started," or, "It is potential." That was not what He proclaimed. When He bore the sins of many, redeemed His bride, and died in the place of His sheep, He cried out, "It is finished!" (John 19:30).

The death of Christ was a real, true, complete satisfaction of divine justice. It was a true payment, an atonement in full—actually, not potentially—made to God by Christ, on behalf of all who would ever believe, because they were chosen by God. The death of Christ was definite, particular, specific, and actual on behalf of God's chosen people. It was limited in extent by the sovereign purposes of God, but unlimited in effect for all who believe.

Atonement is the work of God, and of Christ who accomplished redemption; atonement is not the sinner's work, securing by his own choice a merely possible redemption. Christ conclusively procured salvation for all whom God would call and justify. Sinners do not limit the atonement; God does. On the cross, Jesus actually took the penalty in full for all who would ever believe.

What does that mean for you? First of all, you ought to rejoice, because if you're a believer, the price was paid for you in full. You don't have to activate it. You can't add to it, and you don't have to. You're a trophy of God's divine grace and sovereignty in salvation (Eph 2:7). Secondly, you must evangelize the lost with joy, knowing that there's a holy seed for whom Christ has already died. It is our joy and privilege to be God's instruments to reach them.

But some people will want to know how we can be certain that Christ died for them. The answer is this: If you come and believe in the gospel of the Lord Jesus Christ, then the death of Christ was for you. Don't hang back; simply come at once to Christ.

Some time ago, I was preaching at a conference in London when a preacher pulled me aside and asked, "Do you actually encourage people to come to Christ?" I said, "Yes," to which he responded, "I find it so hard. I'm so restrained in my spirit." If this describes you, then your theology is out of order. We don't know who the elect are, other than those who have already come. We don't know who's been purchased by Christ, awaiting the application of redemption by the Spirit. I answered this preacher, "Paul said, 'We beg you on behalf of Christ' (2 Cor 5:20). Paul said, 'I could wish that I myself were accursed, separated from Christ for the sake of my brethren, my kinsmen according to the flesh' (Rom 9:3), that they might know the Messiah."

So we, like Paul, plead with sinners. We take the gospel to the ends of the earth, and we leave the secret things to the Lord. We follow the responsibility to call sinners to faith, knowing that those who come have had an atonement provided for them in full.

The book of Revelation gives us a glimpse of the body of believers purchased by Christ. In 5:9, we hear a new, heavenly song for the Lamb, who is Christ: "Worthy are You to take the book and to break its seals; for You were slain, and purchased for God with Your blood men from every tribe and tongue and people and nation. You have made them to be a kingdom and priests to our God; and they will reign upon the earth."

It goes on in verses 12–13, "Worthy is the Lamb that was slain to receive power and riches and wisdom and might and honor and glory and blessing.... To Him who sits on the throne, and to the Lamb, be blessing and honor and glory and dominion forever and ever." The elders in verse 14, who represent the church, fall down and worship the Lamb. Worship is the occupation of heaven, and that worship is given to God out of gratitude for His saving plan effected through the sacrifice of Christ.

We see that at the heart of heavenly praise is gratitude for Christ's purchase of sinners for God. As verse 9 says, "Worthy are You to take the book and to break its seals; for You were slain, and purchased for God with Your blood men from every tribe and tongue and people and nation."

All of the redeemed will spend eternity joining in this heavenly song to praise Christ for the perfect, actual atonement He made for sinners like you and me.

EFFECTUAL CALL

"GOD RIDES FORTH CONQUERING IN THE CHARIOT OF HIS GOSPEL; HE CONQUERS THE PRIDE OF THE HEART, AND MAKES THE WILL, WHICH STOOD OUT AS A FORT-ROYAL, TO YIELD AND STOOP TO HIS GRACE."

THOMAS WATSON[25]

A SOVEREIGN SUMMONS

One of the simplest and most common words in the English language is the word *call*. We all understand it, and we frequently use it in conversation. We call our kids to come to dinner and hope they will respond. We call our friends on the phone and hope they will answer. A church will call a pastor and hope he will accept the offer to come and shepherd them.

I remember being called to the principal's office as a kid or receiving a "call slip" to visit the dean's office in college. You may have received a summons from a court, or even a subpoena—a summons commanding a person to appear under a penalty for failure to do so.

There are all kinds of calls, from those less imperative, such as a friendly phone call, to the far more serious call from a church or court subpoena. Each of those calls varies in its significance, and you can choose to ignore and resist any of them.

Scripture, however, reveals a call that cannot be ignored or resisted. It is the unyielding summons from God—a subpoena to appear before Him in His court for the purpose of being declared righteous, having all your sins forgiven, and being set free from all condemnation. This is the divine summons that is referred to as the *effectual call*.

DEFINING THE EFFECTUAL CALL

The Westminster Confession of Faith gives a basic definition of the effectual call:

> All those whom God hath predestinated unto life, and those only, He is pleased, in His appointed and accepted time, effectually to call, by His Word and Spirit, out of that state of sin and death in which they are by nature, to grace and salvation by Jesus Christ: enlightening their minds, spiritually and savingly, to understand the things of God, taking away their heart of stone, and giving unto them an heart of flesh; renewing their wills, and by His almighty power determining them to that which is good; and effectually drawing them to Jesus Christ; yet so as they come most freely, being made willing by His grace.[26]

The doctrine expressed in that paragraph arises from Romans 8, the summary of salvation by Paul:

> We know that God causes all things to work together for good to those who love God, to those who are called according to His purpose. For those whom He foreknew, He also predestined to become conformed to the image of His Son, so that He would be the firstborn among many brethren; and these whom He predestined, He also called; and these whom He called, He also justified; and these whom He justified, He also glorified. (Rom 8:28–30)

In previous chapters, we have addressed the truths of foreknowledge, predestination, justification, and even glorification. But one word that often gets overlooked in those verses, perhaps because we assume we understand it, is "called." Yet it is a concept so definitive to Christian doctrine that verse 28 identifies believers as "those who are *called*."

Paul reveals that this call is limited to those who are the elect—the "predestined." He isn't writing about a broad-sweeping gospel invitation that goes out to the whole world, which is the general or external call of the gospel. As verse 30 makes clear, Paul is talking about the heavenly call that comes irresistibly to the predestined and always results in justification. That is why it is the *effectual* call.

This call is the divine command that brings about justification and glorification. Sinners do not decide independently, in their fallenness, that they will love God. Rather, God decided that we who hated Him would love Him, and then He brought about that love in us by calling us to Himself. First John 4:19 sums up this transformational miracle: "We love [God], because He first loved us."

That call is the summons from the Lord that saves the elect. We love Him solely because He first set His love on us. It is critical that we understand that proper order of events—*He* had to take the initiative to set His love on us, and summon us to salvation.

Romans 9:10–13 helps us understand this call:

> Rebekah also, when she had conceived twins by one man, our father Isaac; for though the twins were not yet born and had not done anything good or bad, so that God's purpose according to His choice would stand, not because of works but because of *Him who calls*, it was said to her, "The older will serve the younger." Just as it is written, "Jacob I loved, but Esau I hated." (emphasis added)

God chose between Jacob and Esau before they were ever born. He chose before they had the opportunity to do any good or evil, so it's erroneous to say His choice depended in any way on their actions or their choice of Him. The fact that these two brothers ended up having very different lives and destinies in God's plan had nothing to do with their own achievements or decisions; it was solely determined by God's sovereign choice. He called one brother and not the other.

Some Christians object to this teaching specifically because they don't like the doctrine of sovereign election or predestination. But we must believe in predestination and effectual calling because they are unequivocally taught in the Bible. Romans 8 and 9 explain these doctrines with unmistakable clarity. Though you may try to explain them away, the Word of God is unbending on these points. We are saved because *He chose* us and *He called* us.

This raises the question of *how* God calls us. Romans 10:13–15 says, "'Whoever will call on the name of the Lord will be saved.' How then will they call on Him in whom they have not believed? How will they believe in Him whom they have not heard? And how will they hear without a preacher? How will they preach unless they are sent?" People cannot believe in a gospel they have never heard. Thus Paul concludes in verse 17, "So faith comes from hearing, and hearing by the word of Christ." Absolutely no one is called by God to salvation apart from the preaching of the gospel, because you must have some understanding of the gospel's truth in order to believe it.

Alongside the external preaching of the gospel, God calls the elect internally by His Spirit. We are born again by the preaching of the Word (1 Pet 1:23) and the power of the Spirit (John 3:5), who recreates us and draws us to God (John 6:44).

This is the call or summons that comes with a divine saving purpose. It comes only to those who are foreknown, predestined, and elect. It is a call that leads through justification to eternal glory. All of that is why theologians have referred to this call as an effective call, a determinative call, a decisive call, a conclusive call, an operative call, and an irresistible call. It is the divine subpoena, not for judgment, but so that a sinner can be declared righteous. It is the effectual call to salvation.

As John Murray explains: "The summons is invested with the efficacy by which we are delivered to the destination intended—we are effectively ushered into the fellowship of Christ. There is something determinate about God's call; by his sovereign power and grace it cannot fail of accomplishment."[27]

THE EXTERNAL CALL

Before defining the effectual call any further, it is important to understand the other primary way the New Testament uses the word *call*. In Matthew 22:14, for example, Jesus says, "Many are called, but few are chosen." That "call" refers to a general invitation for sinners to come to the Lord. "Call" in this context has to do with an external invitation, not an internal work of the Spirit. Many people will hear the gospel preached. Many people are given an invitation to come to Christ. Many will even understand their need for salvation. But only a few are chosen, and they alone receive the internal, effectual call.

It is clear from the context that the call in this passage is an external call. Matthew 22:1–14 records a dramatic parable about a wedding feast. In the parable, a king sends out an invitation to the guests (v. 3), but Jesus says those who were invited "were unwilling to come." Then the king sent out another round of invitations, "but they paid no attention and went their way" (vv. 4–5). Some of those who were invited even killed the messengers who invited them (v. 6). Clearly that call can be rejected.

Finally, the king commanded his slaves to go out and bring in anyone they could find to attend the wedding: "Then [the king] said to his slaves, 'The wedding is ready, but those who were invited were not worthy. Go therefore to the main highways, and as many as you find there, invite to the wedding feast.' Those slaves went out into the streets and gathered together all they found, both evil and good; and the wedding hall was filled with dinner guests" (vv. 8–10).

The parable ends with a strange interaction: "But when the king came in to look over the dinner guests, he saw a man there who was not dressed in wedding clothes, and he said to him, 'Friend, how did you come in here without wedding clothes?' And the man was speechless. Then the king said to the servants, 'Bind him hand and foot, and throw him into the outer darkness; in that place there will be weeping and gnashing of teeth'" (vv. 11–13).

This parable teaches us that there are people who try to enter into the kingdom illegitimately. The man in the parable heard the mass invitation to the wedding but did not actually belong there. The wedding garments in the parable are a reference to the biblical concept of being clothed in righteousness (Job 29:14; Isa 61:10). People who belong in the kingdom are clothed in Christ's righteousness rather than their own (Rom 5:17–18; 2 Cor 5:21; cf. Zech 3:1–5). But this interloper had merely heard the invitation—he heard the external call, but he was not clothed in the righteousness of Christ. Therefore he did not belong at the wedding.

The whole parable is summarized in verse 14, "Many are called, but few are chosen." Many heard the invitation. Many showed up to the wedding. But only a few were chosen.

The man in this parable is like those in Matthew 7:22 who will say to Christ, "Lord, Lord, did we not prophesy in Your name, and in Your name cast out demons, and in Your name perform many miracles?" They have some knowledge of Christ and the gospel. They think they belong in the kingdom. But Christ will respond to them, "I never knew you; depart from Me" (v. 23). They heard an external call, but God never effectually called them to salvation.

While Matthew 22 gives us an illustration of the external call, Romans 8 explains the internal call. We know that Romans 8 does not refer to the external call because verse 30 says, "These whom He predestined, He also called; and these whom He called, He also justified; and these whom He justified, He also glorified." This cannot refer to the external call because all those who are called in Romans 8 are also justified and glorified; as many as are called are also saved. Therefore, this call is effective unto salvation, unlike the external call in Matthew 22.

In summary, the external call is simply that which any person hears, when presented the gospel invitation to come to Christ. By contrast, the internal call is God regenerating a person's heart so as to believe on Christ for salvation.

THE EFFECTUAL CALL IN SCRIPTURE

With these preliminary definitions in mind, we can look at the scope of the word *called* as it is used throughout Scripture.

It's part of a group of words that come out of the root *kaleō*, which means "I call" or "I summon." For example, it is used in Matthew 2:7 when "Herod secretly called the magi." As a king, Herod had the power to summon them to appear before him.

That kind of call had legal implications, but the word is also employed in less formal circumstances. As we have already established, it is so descriptive of Christians that they are frequently referred to as "the called." It is that theological use of the word which is this chapter's focus, and which becomes clear as we consider all that Scripture says about it. So we'll begin with an overview of how the New Testament uses the word "call."

Back in Romans 1:1, Paul labels himself "a bond-servant of Christ Jesus, *called* as an apostle, set apart for the gospel of God" (emphasis added). When the call of God came to the apostle Paul, it was a sovereign, divine, gracious, and irresistible summons. He was slammed to the dirt on the road to Damascus and had no option but to respond (Acts 9:1–19). He was "called" or summoned as an apostle.

In Romans 1:6–7, Paul applies this same idea of calling to his readers. He refers to them as "called of Jesus Christ" and "called as saints." They were called or summoned to be saints in Christ in the same sense that he was called to be an apostle. In both instances, it was solely a work of God.

Paul uses this same terminology in 1 Corinthians 1. In verse 1 he again identifies himself as "Paul, called as an apostle of Jesus Christ by the will of God." Paul's calling was not by man or by his own efforts, but "by the will of God." God summoned him to be an apostle of Jesus Christ. And because God by His will issued it, and by His power accomplished it, this summons was not something Paul could resist.

Paul also calls the Corinthian Christians "those who have been sanctified in Christ Jesus, saints by calling" (v. 2). Clearly, whatever this calling is, it produces a saint. In Romans 8 it leads to justification; here, it leads to sanctification. Verse 9 shows that it also leads to fellowship with Christ: "God is faithful, through whom you were called into fellowship with His Son, Jesus Christ our Lord." So our justification, sanctification, and fellowship with Christ all flow out of God's effectual call to us.

Paul continues in verses 23–24, "We preach Christ crucified, to Jews a stumbling block and to Gentiles foolishness, but to those who are *the called*, both Jews and Greeks, Christ [is] the power of God and the wisdom of God" (emphasis added). Follow the argument here: If you are among "the called," then when Christ is preached, in the moment God has ordained, He will become to you the power of God and the wisdom of God to salvation. In other words, if you are called by God, you will be regenerated. As we saw with Jacob and Esau, the difference between a believer and an unbeliever is solely the call of God. Christians are not more spiritual or inherently better than other people. They are as wretched as any and all other sinners. The only difference is that they have been sovereignly summoned by God to salvation.

In verse 26, Paul encourages the Corinthians to "consider your calling"—recognize their summons from heaven in light of the doctrine of election. He continues, "There were not many wise according to the flesh, not many mighty, not many noble; but God has chosen the foolish things of the world to shame the wise, and God has chosen the weak things of the world to shame the things which are strong, and the base things of the world and the despised God has chosen" (vv. 26–28). The believer's calling is inescapably rooted in the fact that God has chosen who will be saved. Paul presses that point by repeating three times in these verses, "God has chosen."

Verse 30 summarizes, "But by His doing you are in Christ Jesus." This calling into fellowship with Christ comes about "by His doing" alone. Those He sovereignly chose in eternity past, He will sovereignly call to salvation in time.

Paul continues to teach this foundational doctrine in Galatians. Though the Galatians were under assault by false teachers, they were true Christians. So Paul says in Galatians 1:6, "I am amazed that you are so quickly deserting Him who called you by the grace of Christ." His point is that God had summoned them to Himself through the grace of Christ, so it was almost unbelievable that they were wandering away from that to chase after a distorted gospel.

In verses 11–16 the apostle wrote,

> For I would have you know, brethren, that the gospel which was preached by me is not according to man. For I neither received it from man, nor was I taught it, but I received it through a revelation of Jesus Christ.
>
> For you have heard of my former manner of life in Judaism, how I used to persecute the church of God beyond measure and tried to destroy it; and I was advancing in Judaism beyond many of my contemporaries among my countrymen, being more extremely zealous for my ancestral traditions. But ... God, who had set me apart even from my mother's womb and *called me through His grace*, was pleased to reveal His Son in me so that I might preach Him among the Gentiles. (emphasis added)

Paul once sought to kill Christians. That's how passionate he was about Judaism. In his own words: "I was ... extremely zealous for my ancestral traditions." But what brought an end to Paul's rampaging persecution of the church? "[God] called me through His grace." God reached down—because of the determination of His will from before Paul was even in his mother's womb—and called Paul to Himself. Paul understood that God grabbed him by the neck and awakened him to the glory of Christ. This calling Paul experienced was an effectual summons, an irresistible subpoena.

If we continue through Paul's letters, we see this same truth in Ephesians. Ephesians 4:1 says, "I, the prisoner of the Lord, implore you to walk in a manner worthy of the calling with which you have been called." This cannot be a general call to all humanity. Paul is exclusively telling Christians to live in accordance with God's work of saving them, which he describes as "the calling."

Therefore, this calling can only be understood as a calling to salvation. This is a calling into "one body and one Spirit, just as also you were called in one hope of your calling" (v. 4). Whenever the call to salvation is referenced in the New Testament epistles, it always refers to this efficacious, determinative, operative call—it is a *saving* call.

We see the same truth again in Colossians 3:15. This familiar verse states, "Let the peace of Christ rule in your hearts, to which indeed you were called in one body." Here we see that Christians were called into the body of Christ. And we were called to peace through Christ, who now rules in our hearts through His word.

First Thessalonians 2:12 echoes Ephesians 4, "Walk in a manner worthy of the God who calls you into His own kingdom and glory." Again this identifies the call of God into fellowship and relationship with Jesus Christ. In 2 Thessalonians 2:14, Paul writes, "It was for this He called you through our gospel, that you may gain the glory of our Lord Jesus Christ." Whomever the Lord calls, He calls into His Kingdom—to salvation, to faith in the truth, to sanctification by the Spirit, and to eternal glory. This is clearly a saving call.

Second Timothy 1:9 creates a purposeful parallel between calling and salvation. It states, "[God] has saved us and called us with a holy calling." That's two ways of saying the same thing. "He saved us"—which is to say—"[He] called us with a holy calling, not according to our works, but according to His own purpose and grace which was granted us in Christ Jesus from all eternity." Scripture's teaching is unmistakable: God calls whom He predestines from eternity for His own purposes, not because of their works or choices.

Peter explains the same doctrine in his short epistles. First Peter 2:9 states, "You are a chosen race, a royal priesthood, a holy nation, a people for God's own possession, so that you may proclaim the excellencies of Him who has called you out of darkness into His marvelous light."

He references calling again in 3:8–9, "Be harmonious, sympathetic, brotherly, kind-hearted, and humble in spirit; not returning evil for evil or insult for insult, but giving a blessing instead; for you were called for the very purpose that you might inherit a blessing." This call brought you into new life and blessing. To put it another way, this call is effective.

First Peter 5:10 adds, "After you have suffered for a little while, the God of all grace, who called you to His eternal glory in Christ, will Himself perfect, confirm, strengthen and establish you." What a statement! God has called you not only to justification but also to sanctification—to live a godly and virtuous life worthy of your calling. All this culminates in the reality that He has called you to His eternal glory in Christ.

Second Peter 1:2–3 adds, "Grace and peace be multiplied to you in the knowledge of God and of Jesus our Lord; seeing that His divine power has granted to us everything pertaining to life and godliness, through the true knowledge of Him who called us by His own glory and excellence." He called us by His own glory and gave us everything pertaining to life and godliness in Christ.

One final reference that demands our attention appears in Hebrews 3:1, which calls believers "holy brethren, partakers of a heavenly calling." This verse isn't talking about being called to repent by a preacher. It's referring to a divine call. Christians are made to be "holy brethren" because of this heavenly calling.

This verse illuminates the difference between the preacher's call and God's call. The preacher can—he should!—call people to repentance. He must plead with people to come to salvation in Christ. Apostles and prophets have done the same. But that's simply a general outward plea, and it is very different from the inward call that saves—a calling by God's will and power.

When God calls a person, that call necessarily results in that person's salvation. All of the verses discussed here teach us that. As I said, the very use of the word *call* with regard to salvation in the New Testament epistles refers not to a general outward call, but to an efficacious, saving act of God. That call is an unyielding summons from God that a person *will* respond to. That is why theologians have labeled it *irresistible grace*.

But I'm not convinced that's the most biblical title for this doctrine.

IRRESISTIBLE GRACE OR EFFECTUAL CALL?

It is true that God's grace is effective to accomplish God's purposes and, therefore, cannot be resisted. So I understand why many people use the term *irresistible grace*. But I prefer not to use it for three reasons.

First, *irresistible* has negative connotations. I would rather this matter be clearly understood as a positive work of God rather than a negative work of man—it's not about what *man can't* do; it's about what *God can* do. Second, "irresistible grace" is redundant. God's acts of grace are always unilateral and, by definition, irresistible; if God decides to be gracious, that grace is backed by His unstoppable power.

Third and perhaps most importantly, the familiar term underdefines the nature of this grace. The Bible describes it as a heavenly calling, a calling to holiness, a calling to sanctification, a calling to justification, a calling to communion with the saints, and a calling into the body of Christ. As a label, *irresistible grace* simply falls short of the grandeur of this doctrine. Ephesians 2:8–9 says, "By grace you have been saved through faith; and that not of yourselves, it is the gift of God; not as a result of works, so that no one may boast." The whole of our salvation is a gift of God's grace. I love how Philippians 1:29 puts it: "To you it has been granted for Christ's sake, not only to believe in Him, but also to suffer for His sake." Your belief in Christ has been granted to you by God as a gift, not as something we might seek to resist.

All of this is why I prefer the term *effectual call*—it conveys the idea of a sovereign summons. *Effectual call* emphasizes God's unyielding work, rather than man's resistance. I know that messes up the traditional TULIP acronym, but that's OK. This is still the same doctrine that the *I* in TULIP denotes.

Man cannot resist God's saving will. Regardless, in naming this doctrine I prefer to put the emphasis on God's power rather than man's resistance. Still, whatever the terms, this doctrine raises the question of man's will in salvation. If the call to salvation cannot be resisted, how does the human will fit into the design?

WHAT ABOUT FREE WILL?

God has predetermined from eternity past to save certain people (Eph 1:4). Then He reaches out inside time to save them through issuing His effectual call, which lifts them out of darkness and unbelief (1 Pet 2:9). God exercises His power to make the elect sinner come into His court to be justified, that they may be ultimately eternally glorified. This is God's sovereign, saving call, testified to throughout the New Testament, as we've just seen.

But you're probably already aware that this doctrine bothers some people. They say, "It is not right to say God is going to bring sinners to Himself kicking and screaming. It's wrong to say that you can't fight or resist God's grace. God would never overpower your will and violate your freedom."

In the place of the effectual call, they say God merely makes strong suggestions. He may be very persuasive, and we can pray that He would open people's minds and remove their blindness, but—they argue—God would never force anyone to be saved. We can ask God to give them opportunity, but in the end, the final choice belongs to the sinner.

One notable scholar who is helpful on many other topics, Norman Geisler, attacks this doctrine in a book titled *Chosen But Free*. He argues that irresistible grace or effectual calling makes God into a dictator whose power crushes our freedom by dragging us into His kingdom.[28]

All such objections are commonplace but also needless because they mischaracterize what Scripture says. No one is coerced into the kingdom. No one has ever been saved against his will—and no one ever will be. It is an act of the will to believe. Everybody who is saved is saved because they chose to believe the gospel, willed to believe it with all their heart and soul. No one is ever saved without being willing.

But the key question is, *What made them willing?* Was it the preacher, by smashing their resistance to the gospel with persuasive preaching? Was it the sinner who himself simply chose to believe? After all, that's the necessary conclusion in a system that idolizes free will: that in the end, the sinner became willing by pulling himself up by his own bootstraps, out of unwillingness.

One verse that helps us understand this issue is Psalm 110:3. The psalmist writes, "Thy people shall be willing in the day of thy power" (KJV). No sinner is ever going to be willing until the power of God transforms him. There's nothing in the sinner to make him willing, and there's nothing, even in the best preacher's efforts, that can transform a sinner's fallen will. It is only when the power of God makes him willing that he becomes willing. This is exactly what we learned when we examined the doctrine of absolute inability.

Unregenerate sinners are absolutely unable to choose to believe the gospel. Romans 3:10–11 says, "There is none righteous, not even one; there is none who understands, there is none who seeks for God." Those two verses alone should clarify the issue. Not a single sinner "seeks for God." But Paul continues in the next verse, "All have turned aside, together they have become useless; there is none who does good, there is not even one" (v. 12).

That sad condition describes everyone in their fallen state. On their own, no one is willing or able to trust Christ for salvation. But why? Ephesians 2:1–3 paints a vivid picture:

> You were dead in your trespasses and sins, in which you formerly walked according to the course of this world, according to the prince of the power of the air, of the spirit that is now working in the sons of disobedience. Among them we too all formerly lived in the lusts of our flesh, indulging the

> desires of the flesh and of the mind, and were by nature children of wrath, even as the rest.

That is a description of all of us before God regenerates us and gives us a redeemed will: We were hopeless because dead people can't respond.

First Corinthians 2:14 clarifies even further, "A natural man does not accept the things of the Spirit of God, for they are foolishness to him; and he cannot understand them, because they are spiritually appraised." That neatly sums up what we mean by *absolute inability*. The sinner "does not" and "cannot" accept spiritual truth.

No sinner left to himself is willing to understand, repent, believe, and choose God or choose salvation. The corruption of sin is far too profound and spiritually systemic. The sinner becomes willing only in the day of divine power (Ps 110:3). God must summon us by His sovereign power—He must make us willing.

Yet it's not as if the sinner comes protesting and trying to resist God's call. Lost sinners do have freedom of the will, which simply means they are free to choose what they want. But they only ever choose sin because they only ever *want* sin.

Jonathan Edwards explains that the will is always informed by the mind: "Every act of the will is some way connected with the understanding .... the soul always wills or chooses that which, in the present view of the mind ... appears most agreeable."[29] People always choose what they think is best—but their thinking is corrupted by sin.

Like the will, the mind is not neutral. It is corrupt. Ephesians 4:17–18 says that unbelievers live "in the futility of their mind, being darkened in their understanding, excluded from the life of God because of the ignorance that is in them, because of the hardness of their heart." So we are all free to choose what our mind thinks is best, but apart from God, our mind is corrupted such that it thinks sin is best.

When the sinner is presented with the gospel, he will not naturally think that repenting of sin and believing on Christ is best. The unregenerate sinner's will is never to choose righteousness or God. Nothing is stopping him, but his mind doesn't regard belief in the gospel as desirable. Unless God changes the way we think, our mind will always tell us to rebel against God and the gospel—which is precisely what we do.

But when the divine summons comes, the sinner is *made* to be willing. When God effectually calls a sinner to salvation, the sinner is eager to respond. In salvation, we have freedom of the will just as we do before salvation. But instead of choosing sin, we choose Christ. It is this understanding of the freedom of the will which leads me to prefer the term *effectual call* over *irresistible grace*.

This understanding of the freedom of the will also gives proper primacy to God's will over man's. God's will is determinative in salvation; man's will is reactive. Remember John 1:12–13, "As many as received Him, to them He gave the right to become children of God, even to those who believe in His name, who were born, not of blood nor of the will of the flesh nor of the will of man, but of God." Christians are born again not of their own will, but of God's.

Romans 9:15–16 also shows us the place of our wills in relation to God's. Paul writes, "[God] says to Moses, 'I will have mercy on whom I have mercy, and I will have compassion on whom I have compassion.' So then it does not depend on the man who wills or the man who runs, but on God who has mercy." Again, Scripture is clear that it is not man's will which initiates salvation. It is God's. That logically follows, because no sinner chooses Christ unless God has first regenerated his will.

No one chooses to believe the gospel until God calls and regenerates him. This is why we must affirm that faith in Christ comes after regeneration and the effectual call. First John 5:1 puts it, "Whoever believes that Jesus is the Christ is born of God." The verb translated "is born of God" is in the perfect tense and is more accurately translated "has been born of God."[30]

The point is clear that a person believes on Christ only if he has already been born of God. The regenerate will and mind joyfully choose to believe the gospel only after God has worked in them. Unregenerate, we will only choose sin. But as soon as we are born again, our regenerate mind understands the goodness of Christ and our regenerate will chooses to believe on Him for salvation. This is why we must acknowledge that regeneration through God's effectual calling precedes faith. Importantly, this understanding also shows us that God's effectual call is not *against* our will, but before it and with it.

EXAMPLES OF THE SAVING CALL

God's saving call is described throughout Scripture, especially in the epistles. But the book of Acts gives us illustrations of what it looks like in a person's life. Acts puts the new birth and effectual call on display in real time.

Acts 13:48 tells us a certain group of Gentiles "began rejoicing and glorifying the word of the Lord." Why did this specific group receive the gospel? The second half of this verse explains, "As many as had been appointed to eternal life believed." Those whom God appointed to salvation were in that moment called out of their ignorance. We know the Lord had to call them because of what we saw in Romans 3:11: "There is none who seeks for God." This scene in Acts illustrates for us the efficacious call performed by the power of God. Their rejoicing is the fruit of an internal call executed by the power of God that brought them into truth, repentance, faith, and life eternal.

Acts 16:14 introduces us to a woman named Lydia and describes her as "a worshiper of God." This means that she'd turned from Greek paganism to the God of Israel. But she had not yet believed the gospel unto salvation. But as Paul was preaching in that region, Luke records that Lydia "was listening" to his external call.

Lydia listened to the gospel, but as we saw from Matthew 22, not everyone who listens to the gospel believes. At the very end of the book of Acts, Paul quotes from Isaiah 6:9–10,

> You will keep on hearing, but will not understand; and you will keep on seeing, but will not perceive; for the heart of this people has become dull, and with their ears they scarcely hear, and they have closed their eyes; otherwise they might see with their eyes, and hear with their ears, and understand with their heart and return, and I would heal them. (Acts 28:26–27)

Many unbelievers will hear the external call of the gospel but not respond. Just as Jesus explained, "Why do you not understand what I am saying? It is because you cannot hear My word" (John 8:43). They may hear externally, but not in an internal or saving way.

So what was different about Lydia? Acts 16:14 says, "*The Lord opened her heart to respond to the things spoken by Paul*" (emphasis added). That is the efficacious call. It wasn't that Lydia was wiser than anyone else or that she moved herself to accept the gospel; it was the work of the Lord in summoning her to believe. This is exactly what Jesus taught in John 6:44, "No one can come to Me *unless the Father who sent Me draws him*" (emphasis added).

In Acts 13:48 we saw the external fruit of God's internal call. But Lydia's testimony gives us a peek into the inner workings of God's effectual call. The Lord opens the mind and the heart, and the one who is unwilling becomes willing. It is an act of His grace. That's why Acts 18:27 says unbelievers "believed through grace." Apart from God's gracious, effective call of sinners to Himself, they would never believe—and Lydia is one of the clearest examples of this reality.

Perhaps the most dramatic example of God's efficacious call was in the life of the apostle Paul. His conversion story is one of the greatest stories in human history. Its repetition multiple times in the book of Acts (9:1–20; 22:1–16; 26:9–18) indicates its importance.

It is fitting that Paul's conversion would be unique because he was such a unique individual—by birth, a Jew; by conviction, a Pharisee; by citizenship, a Roman; by education, a Greek; and then by grace, a Christian (Phil 3:2–7). He became a missionary, theologian, evangelist, teacher, preacher, and indispensable leader in the early church—all at the same time. There has never been another man quite like him. And because of his great significance, it's no exaggeration to say that the conversion of this man was the hinge on which the future of the church turned.

But to fully understand his conversion, we have to remember where he started. Luke first introduces Paul in Acts 7. In this chapter, a deacon named Stephen preached an evangelistic sermon that traced the history of the Old Testament and culminated in the arrival of Jesus the Messiah who was ultimately crucified (vv. 51–53).

Stephen was a faithful evangelist to the Hellenistic synagogues, and this sermon was specifically tailored for a Jewish audience, to convict them of betraying their Messiah. But the message was poorly received, and they stoned Stephen to death. As they took up the stones to murder him, verse 58 records, "The witnesses laid aside their robes at the feet of a young man named Saul." Paul, still called Saul in this passage, "was in hearty agreement" with Stephen's murder (8:1).

In fact, we know Paul was the execution's orchestrator and overseer by the fact that people laid their cloaks at his feet. Acts 8:1 continues, "And on that day a great persecution began against the church in Jerusalem [that scattered Christians] throughout the regions of Judea and Samaria." All of this happened under the supervision of Paul.

The apostle describes himself as formerly "a persecutor of the church" (Phil 3:6). In 1 Timothy 1:13 he writes, "I was formerly a blasphemer and a persecutor and a violent aggressor." Luke continues in Acts 8:3, "Saul began ravaging the church, entering house after house, and dragging off men and women, he would put them in prison." Later in the book of Acts, Paul recounts the details of his violent behavior.

> I thought to myself that I had to do many things hostile to the name of Jesus of Nazareth. And this is just what I did in Jerusalem; not only did I lock up many of the saints in prisons, having received authority from the chief priests, but also when they were being put to death I cast my vote against them. And as I punished them often in all the synagogues, I tried to force them to blaspheme; and being furiously enraged at them, I kept pursuing them even to foreign cities. (Acts 26:9–11)

This is Paul. Persecutor. Violent aggressor. Murderer. One who savaged the body of Christ.

But ravaging Jerusalem wasn't enough for him. After successfully purging the city of those he believed to be heretics, he decided he would chase down those outside Jerusalem also. He wanted to stamp them out wherever they were. So when he heard that a group of them had gone to Damascus, he secured permission from the religious elites to continue the purge there. All of this leads to the great moment of his conversion in Acts 9:1–16.

> Now Saul, still breathing threats and murder against the disciples of the Lord, went to the high priest, and asked for letters from him to the synagogues at Damascus, so that if he found any belonging to the Way, both men and women, he might bring them bound to Jerusalem. As he was traveling, it happened that he was approaching Damascus, and suddenly a light from heaven flashed around him; and he fell to the ground and heard a voice saying to him, "Saul, Saul, why are you persecuting Me?" And he said, "Who are You, Lord?" And He said, "I am Jesus whom you are persecuting, but get up and enter the city, and it will be told you what you must do." The men who traveled with him stood speechless, hearing the voice but seeing no one. Saul got up from the ground, and though his eyes were open, he could see nothing; and leading him by the hand, they brought him into Damascus. And he was three days without sight, and neither ate nor drank.
>
> Now there was a disciple at Damascus named Ananias; and the Lord said to him in a vision, "Ananias." And he said, "Here I am, Lord." And the Lord said to him, "Get up and go to the street called Straight, and inquire at the house of Judas for a man from Tarsus named Saul, for he is praying, and he has seen in a vision a man named Ananias come in and lay his hands on

> him, so that he might regain his sight." But Ananias answered, "Lord, I have heard from many about this man, how much harm he did to Your saints at Jerusalem; and here he has authority from the chief priests to bind all who call on Your name." But the Lord said to him, "Go, for he is a chosen instrument of Mine, to bear My name before the Gentiles and kings and the sons of Israel; for I will show him how much he must suffer for My name's sake."

This was a radical change of plans for Paul. It wasn't like he thought it over and eventually came to the conclusion that his deeds were wicked and he needed a savior. It happened in a moment because it was an act of God. Verse 3 says, "As he was traveling, it happened that he was approaching Damascus, and *suddenly* a light from heaven flashed around him" (emphasis added).

We know that all people who are saved are saved because of a sovereign work of God. But not all of them have this kind of experience—I certainly did not. God calls each one of us to Himself, but this call is usually indiscernible to our senses. It is an *internal* call. But in the case of Paul, Scripture gives us the full story of both the internal and external call.

Acts 9:3 gives us just enough detail to know that the calling of Paul was from heaven, but Paul gives more details when he retells this testimony later. Acts 22:6 tells us that this event happened at noon, when the sun was at its apex. If you've ever stood beneath the Middle Eastern sun at noon, you understand its extreme strength.

The light from heaven, however, eclipsed even the scorching midday sun in its brightness. The sun is bright but distant; this greater light was in their very midst. As this light from heaven flashed around them, the whole group collapsed to the ground in sheer terror (26:14). This miraculous, supernatural light outshone the sun and terrified the group who saw it.

While the others were stupefied and confused, Paul saw and heard Jesus (9:4, 7; cf. 1 Cor 15:8). He saw the glorified Christ. Immediately, Paul knew he was speaking to God; that's why he asks, "Who are you *Lord*?" (Acts 9:5). He was broken and penitent now, lying beneath the conquering Christ and in need of mercy. His conversion was shocking and sudden. God erased all his doubts, and he knew the truth immediately.

In fact, Paul's conversion was so immediate and dramatic that it has always puzzled some historians and commentators. A few have suggested that the hot sun got to his head or some other weather phenomena scared him. Others suggest that his sudden change of conviction was caused by a stroke or other health issues. All of those ideas ignore the explanation clearly given in Scripture. Acts 9 tells us the external testimony of what happened, but Paul tells us the internal testimony in 1 Timothy 1:12–16:

> I thank Christ Jesus our Lord, who has strengthened me, because He considered me faithful, putting me into service, even though I was formerly a blasphemer and a persecutor and a violent aggressor. Yet I was shown mercy because I acted ignorantly in unbelief; and the grace of our Lord was more than

> abundant, with the faith and love which are found in Christ Jesus. It is a trustworthy statement, deserving full acceptance, that Christ Jesus came into the world to save sinners, among whom I am foremost of all. Yet for this reason I found mercy, so that in me as the foremost, Jesus Christ might demonstrate His perfect patience as an example for those who would believe in Him for eternal life.

That's the internal testimony. Paul's life changed, not because he thought it over and decided to follow Christ but because he "was shown mercy." That is a magnificent picture of divine salvation.

If you ever doubt the sovereignty of God in salvation, those doubts should disappear when you hear Paul's story. He is the classic case which proves God to be the initiator of salvation. Before he was called by God, Paul lived for two purposes: to uphold false religion and to destroy the body of Christ. But he was transformed—radically, instantaneously, and permanently.

It is important to remember that Paul had heard the gospel before that moment of salvation. We know this because no one is ever saved apart from the preaching of the gospel (Rom 10:14–17). Paul was well aware of Jesus' claim to be the Messiah and the exclusive way of salvation. He may even have heard Stephen's sermon in Acts 7. In other words, Paul had heard an *external* call before this moment on the Damascus Road. But this conversion story shows us the *internal* call of salvation—the effectual call Paul describes in his letters.

Paul was sovereignly called because he was appointed to salvation and apostleship by God (Acts 22:14). Paul was going one way, and God sovereignly spun him around because He had elected him before the foundation of the world.

This is what takes place every time a person responds to the gospel in faith and repentance. No one is ever saved because he comes to his senses or because he is persuaded by clever preaching or an emotional appeal. That is an illusion. People are saved because God summons them. The gospel alone is what God uses to awaken the sinner, and He makes the sinner willing to believe.

Just as Paul the persecutor was called to be an apostle, each one of us who has been saved was called from darkness into light. God sovereignly calls the sinner as the object of His electing grace and regenerating power. It doesn't happen as dramatically as Paul's conversion, but it is always a sovereign act of God.

A FALSE CONFIDENCE

I am blessed to have been a member of a group of Christians called the Alliance of Confessing Evangelicals, a formidable group of theologians around America. In 1996, this group put out what is called the Cambridge Declaration, which said, among other things, "Unwarranted confidence in human ability is a product of fallen human nature."[31] The only reason we think we can make ourselves willing to be saved is because our thinking is corrupt.

The declaration goes on to say,

> This false confidence now fills the evangelical world; from the self-esteem gospel, to the health and wealth gospel, from those who have transformed the gospel into a product to be sold and sinners into consumers who want to buy, to others who treat Christian faith as being true simply because it works.... God's grace in Christ is not merely necessary but is the sole efficient cause of salvation. We confess that human beings are born spiritually dead and are incapable even of cooperating with regenerating grace.

Then it adds,

> We reaffirm that in salvation we are rescued from God's wrath by his grace alone. It is the supernatural work of the Holy Spirit that brings us to Christ by releasing us from our bondage to sin and raising us from spiritual death to spiritual life.
>
> We deny that salvation is in any sense a human work. Human methods, techniques or strategies by themselves cannot accomplish this transformation. Faith is not produced by our unregenerated human nature.

This is the truth of the gospel. And when we overestimate the ability of man to choose God, we undervalue God's saving call to men. Even anti-Calvinist theologians have recognized the importance of this doctrine.

Charles Wesley was anything but a Calvinist. He wrote many hymns from an anti-Calvinist viewpoint—believing in the freedom of the will or the ability of the sinner to choose God. But sometimes he wrote better than his theology allowed.

You'll recognize these lines from his hymn "And Can It Be?":

> Long my imprisoned spirit lay
> fast bound in sin and nature's night;
> Thine eye diffused a quick'ning ray,
> I woke, the dungeon flamed with light.
> My chains fell off, my heart was free;
> I rose, went forth and followed Thee.

That sounds like it was written by a Calvinist! Sinners are prisoners in darkness, and until God shined the light and broke your chains, nothing about that could change. Unless God sent out the summons, the prisoner would never be free. This is the essence of this great truth—all the glory goes to God.

THE NECESSITY OF THE EFFECTUAL CALL

You've probably noticed at this point that the doctrines of grace all rely on one another. In previous chapters, we've already covered the doctrines of absolute inability, divine election, and actual atonement. Just as these other doctrines inform the effectual call, the effectual call fits in seamlessly with these other doctrines.

We have seen already that the effectual call is necessary because of man's absolute inability. Men who are dead in sin would never turn and believe the gospel unless God sovereignly summoned them to Himself (John 6:44). The doctrine of the effectual call ensures that men will believe on Christ in God's plan of salvation.

The doctrine of divine election refers to God's work in eternity past. Ephesians 1:4 says God "chose us in Him before the foundation of the world." So this act of God in selecting who will be saved happened before anyone was born. On the other hand, the effectual call is the act of God in time drawing sinners to Himself. Believers are elected unto salvation in the past but summoned to Christ in the present (John 6:65). The effectual call brings the doctrine of election into fruition.

The relationship between actual atonement and the effectual call is seen in John 10. Verse 3 says the Good Shepherd, who is Christ, "calls his own sheep by name." This is an image of the effectual call. The Good Shepherd calls His sheep to Himself, by their individual names, to come and follow Him. In the same way Jesus calls each believer out of deadness into new life.

Then in verse 11, Jesus says, "I am the good shepherd; the good shepherd lays down His life for the sheep." The shepherd didn't lay down His life for just any sheep. He sacrificed Himself for *His* sheep, the very sheep which He called by name. The sheep that the

Father gave the Son in election (v. 29) are the same sheep that the Son calls to Himself through the effectual call (v. 3) and the same sheep the Son died for in the atonement (v. 11). This is exactly what we saw in Romans 8. The same group that is predestined is also called, justified, and glorified (vv. 29–31).

When we see all these doctrines lined up next to each other, it becomes clear that God alone is the author of salvation from beginning to end. He elects. He makes atonement. He calls dead sinners to life. All of this is done "to the praise of His glory" (Eph 1:12, 14; cf. v. 6).

Everything God does, He does for His own glory, and our salvation is no different. It is only by the doctrines of grace that God's glory in salvation is preserved, because only the doctrines of grace give all the credit for salvation to Him. That is why the Reformers defended these doctrines and summarized them in the phrase *Soli Deo Gloria* ("to the glory of God alone"). Our salvation, like everything else, can be attributed to God alone so that it brings Him alone glory.

AMAZING GRACE

It was a privilege to have James Montgomery Boice preach at Grace Community Church over the years. He was a great preacher as well as a mentor to me, and his many books are still a blessing.

He wrote in one of his books about John Newton, the author of "Amazing Grace,"

> Newton was raised in a Christian home in which he was taught verses of the Bible, but his mother died when he was only six years old and he was sent to live with a relative who hated the Bible and mocked Christianity. Newton ran away to sea. He was wild in those years and was known for being able to swear for two hours without repeating himself. He was forced to enlist in the British navy, but he deserted, was captured, and was beaten publicly as a punishment. Eventually Newton got into the merchant marine and went to Africa. In his memoirs he wrote that he went to Africa for one reason only, "that I might sin my fill."
>
> Newton fell in with a Portuguese slave trader, in whose home he was cruelly treated. This man often went away on slaving expeditions, and when he was gone his power passed to his African wife, the chief woman of his harem. She hated all white men and vented her hatred on Newton. He says that for months he was forced to grovel in the dirt, eating his food from the ground like a dog. He was beaten mercilessly if he touched it. In time, thin and emaciated, Newton made his way to the sea, where he was picked up by a British ship making its way up the coast to England.
>
> When the captain of the ship learned that the young man knew something about navigation as a result of being in the British Navy, he made him a ship's mate. But even then Newton fell into

trouble. One day, when the captain was ashore, Newton broke out the ship's supply of rum and got the crew drunk. He was so drunk himself that when the captain returned and struck him on the head, Newton fell overboard and would have drowned if one of the sailors had not quickly hauled him back on board.

Near the end of one voyage, as they were approaching Scotland, the ship ran into bad weather and was blown off course. Water poured in, and the ship began to sink. The young profligate was sent down into the hold to pump water. The storm lasted for days. Newton was terrified. He was sure the ship would sink and he would drown. But in the hold of the ship, as he desperately pumped water, the God of all grace, whom he had tried to forget but who had never forgotten him, brought to his mind Bible verses he had learned in his home as a child. The way of salvation opened up to him. He was born again and deeply transformed. Much later, when he was again in England, Newton began to study theology and eventually became a preacher, first in a little town called Olney and later in London.

Of this storm William Cowper, the British poet who became a fast personal friend of Newton and lived with him for several years, wrote:

> God moves in a mysterious way,
> His wonders to perform;
> He plants his footsteps in the sea
> And rides upon the storm.

> And so he does! Newton was a great preacher of grace, for he had learned that where sin increased, grace abounded all the more (Rom. 5:20). He is proof that the grace of God is sufficient to save anybody, and that he saves them by grace alone.[32]

We know that when John Newton wrote, "Amazing grace, how sweet the sound," he was talking about that moment in the bottom of the ship when he heard the saving call of God's grace. Believers ever since have been singing of God's amazing, summoning grace that saves wretches like us. This great truth that Newton wrote about should thrill our hearts to the very core—God has stooped down and personally summoned each one of us to salvation.

THE COMFORT OF CALLING

When you study your Bible in the future, I hope the word *called* jumps off the page at you. God's calling of believers is not wishful or hopeful, like our calling of other people to repent and believe. It's not like calling the kids for dinner or calling a friend on the phone. It is an efficacious, effectual, determinative, operative, and saving call.

If you are a Christian, God has "called you out of darkness into His marvelous light" (1 Pet 2:9). He didn't call you out of darkness and then wait to see what would happen. He actually brought you from one place to another. He drew you to Himself. That's why theologians throughout the centuries have called this the effectual or saving call. It's not a casual request; it is a divine summons. This truth, contained in all the Scriptures we looked at, is not obscure or confusing.

Instead of being a controversial doctrine, the effectual call should be a comfort for all believers. Romans 8:28, a verse you probably have memorized, says, "We know that God causes all things to work together for good to those who love God, to those who are called according to His purpose."

What does it mean that "all things ... work together for good"? Simply put, nothing happens to believers except what God has planned for their greatest good. Whatever believers face in this life is God's providential care for them. This does not mean that "all things" are good in themselves, but they work together for our ultimate good—our sanctification and future hope (vv. 29–30).

And to whom does this wonderful promise apply? Paul says it belongs to "those who love God" and "those who are called according to His purpose" (v. 28). God works all things together for the ultimate good of those He planned to save in eternity past and called to salvation in their lifetime (v. 29). If God has called you to salvation, you can rest in the fact that He has also arranged every aspect of your life.

Some people believe this promise but still fear that God may change His mind at some point. What if I'm too sinful? Will God ever remove His calling of me? Romans 11:29 says, "The gifts and the calling of God are irrevocable." God will never repeal

His calling of anyone. He never repents or regrets calling anyone to salvation.

Men make covenants and break them all the time. People get married and publicly make vows, only to violate them. But God has perfect integrity in everything He does, and this is cause for all Christians to rejoice. God will never reverse His saving call. If you have been called by God, you will make it all the way to glorification (cf. 8:30). It is little wonder why Paul ends Romans chapter 11 in doxology: "To Him be the glory forever. Amen" (v. 36).

As the psalmist wrote in Psalm 4:8, "In peace I will both lie down and sleep, for You alone, O Lord, make me to dwell in safety." Every Christian should have this peace. God calls us, works all things for our good, and never goes back on His saving work in us. It grieves me to think that Christians miss out on this peace because they don't understand this or the other doctrines of grace.

Finally, this wonderful and comforting doctrine should cause us to live faithfully for Christ. In Ephesians 4:1 Paul says, "I, the prisoner of the Lord, implore you to walk in a manner worthy of the calling with which you have been called, with all humility and gentleness, with patience, showing tolerance for one another in love, being diligent to preserve the unity of the Spirit in the bond of peace."

I remember a man told me when I was in seminary, "The whole Christian life is simply becoming what you are." That's the truth.

We were called to salvation, and our Christian life is the journey of living up to that calling.

That's what Paul means when he says you must "walk in a manner worthy of the calling with which you have been called." The idea of a "walk" is used in Scripture as a description of our daily conduct. Paul uses this same metaphor in verse 17, where he tells the Ephesians not to "walk" like unsaved people. Our walk is our daily conduct and lifestyle. The word "worthy" is translated from an interesting Greek word. It literally means that something is "equivalent." You can imagine scales being perfectly balanced with the same amount of weight on each side.

So Paul's command is for Christians to bring all of their conduct into congruity with their heavenly calling to salvation. This is a command to live a life that is in perfect balance and harmony with your position in Christ. It isn't enough to merely study and understand these doctrines of grace. We must also labor to live a life consistent with the calling we have received from God.

One man who embodied this lifelong labor to live consistently with God's effectual call is William Wilberforce, that great Christian leader who led the charge against slavery in England. His personal journals have been published, and they exhibit an obsession with sanctification that we should all strive to emulate. I think this one entry of his is a fitting conclusion to this study on the effectual call:

> To Thee, O God, I fly through the Savior; enable me to live more worthy of my holy calling; to be more useful and efficient, that my time may not be frittered away unprofitably to myself and others, but that I really may be of use in my generation, and adorn the doctrine of God my Savior.... I am a poor, helpless creature, Lord, strengthen me.[33]

May God give every one of us the same resolve to understand God's effectual call and to live a life consistent with it.

PERSEVERING FAITH

"THOUGH YOU TAKE BUT WEAK AND FAINT HOLD ON CHRIST, HE TAKES SURE, STRONG, AND UNCONQUERABLE HOLD ON YOU."

JOHN OWEN[34]

TO THE END

Salvation is meaningless if it isn't eternal.

All the other doctrines of salvation, from election to glorification, are voided if salvation isn't secure forever.

This truth is often referred to as "eternal security," "once saved, always saved," or "the perseverance of the saints." And of course, all of those phrases apply—true believers are secure and will persevere in faith to the end.

Scripture teaches that the elect are kept by God, who has given them a faith that perseveres, therefore He deserves all the glory for our salvation. It is a doctrine so plainly taught in God's Word that past generations of the church have consistently affirmed it in the clearest possible terms.

PERSEVERANCE HISTORICALLY DEFINED

The year was 1643. The place, the Jerusalem Chamber of Westminster Abbey. There gathered the best theological minds and greatest biblical scholars in England. The Puritans were the dominating force among them—lovers of Christ, Scripture, and the truth.

These Puritans gathered together, about a hundred strong with lords and commoners intermingled, and endeavored to produce a robust and comprehensive doctrinal statement. After years of intense study of Scripture, dialogue, scholastic effort, and discussion, they completed their task in 1646 and produced the Westminster Confession of Faith.

Well-known Puritans like Thomas Goodwin, James Ussher, John Lightfoot, Samuel Rutherford, Jeremiah Burroughs, and the chairman of the group, William Twisse, labored to produce this seminal Christian creed.

Among the confession's many statements is one about the security of salvation. This principle, they were convinced, is what the Bible teaches. But they gave it a far more accurate designation: "the perseverance of the saints."[35]

Their summary of this great doctrine is a brief and unambiguous declaration. The confession says,

> They, whom God hath accepted in His beloved [Son], effectually called and sanctified by His Spirit, can neither totally nor finally fall away from the state of grace; but shall certainly persevere therein to the end, and be eternally saved.[36]

As we will see in this chapter, this statement is biblically accurate and, frankly, needs no amending. The Westminster Assembly got it right.

Nor was it as if they had to look very long to find passages of Scripture supporting their statement. There is a mountain of biblical evidence for this doctrine. But we will have a clearer understanding of what the perseverance of the saints *does* mean if we look first at what it does *not* mean.

WHAT PERSEVERANCE IS NOT

Perseverance does not mean that Christians never fail. Christians do fail, severely and repeatedly, throughout their lives. Perseverance means believers, in the words of the Westminster Confession, "can neither totally nor finally fall away from the state of grace."[37]

Do we fail? Yes. Do we fail severely? Yes. Do we fail repeatedly? Yes. Can we fail completely? No. Can we fail finally? *No.*

The Westminster Confession goes on to say,

> Nevertheless they may, through the temptations of Satan and of the world, the prevalency of corruption remaining in them, and the neglect of the means of their perseverance, fall into grievous sins; and for a time continue therein: whereby they incur God's displeasure, and grieve His Holy Spirit; come to be deprived of some measure of their graces and comforts; have their hearts hardened, and their consciences wounded; hurt and scandalize others, and bring temporal judgments upon themselves.[38]

The confession's writers understood that perseverance does not mean perfection. We persevere, but we are not perfect. There is corruption remaining in us. We can neglect the means of grace, stumble into grievous sin, continue in sin for a time, incur God's displeasure, grieve the Spirit, and bring upon ourselves the deprivation of some measures of grace and comfort. We hurt others in the church and bring upon ourselves temporal judgments and disciplines.

We're not talking about reaching a state of sinlessness. We're talking about enduring in faith *despite failing*. Contrary to what some teach, sinless perfection is not attainable in this life. The failures the confession mentions here describe all of us to one degree or another.

Secondly, perseverance does not mean that anyone who professes faith in Christ can live any way they like with no fear of hell.

It is not enough to have a superficial faith in Christ. It is not enough to have good feelings about Jesus and a shallow interest or momentary commitment to Him. That is why the better descriptor for this doctrine is *the perseverance of the saints* rather than *eternal security*. It is not just that we are eternally secure; it is that we are eternally secure because our faith perseveres.

This is why Jesus says, "If you continue in My word, then you are truly disciples of Mine" (John 8:31). True disciples continue in faith—and they don't behave like nonbelievers. In fact, you can recognize them by their fruit (Matt 7:20; see also John 15:1–11). Ephesians 2:8–9 says, "By grace you have been saved through faith; and that not of yourselves, it is the gift of God; not as a result of works, so that no one may boast." But even though your salvation is not of works, the *result* of your salvation is good works. That is why Paul continues in verse 10, "For we are His workmanship, created in Christ Jesus for good works, which God prepared beforehand so that we would walk in them."

A professing believer who lives a sinful, unrepentant life but has no fear of hell because he thinks he's eternally secure is a person who is deeply delusional. That is why we don't talk about the doctrine of eternal security as if it meant that one rote prayer or confession leads to a true salvation forever secure.[39]

To speak of the security of the believer is not in itself wrong—we are secure. But *perseverance of the saints* is more accurate because it is not as if someone were secure no matter how much they live in sin, turn against Christ, or even flatly deny Him. Rather, security is a reality because of persevering faith. A believer may sin—again, even seriously and repeatedly—but he will not forsake his faith in Christ. He will not become an unbeliever who falls under the utter domination of sin.

First John 3:10 states this reality in the clearest possible terms: "By this the children of God and the children of the devil are obvious: anyone who does not practice righteousness is not of God." It's that simple. Anyone who does not practice righteousness is not of God. The prior verse says, "No one who is born of God practices sin." Sin cannot be the unbroken pattern of a believer's life.

The doctrine of perseverance, then, is this: At salvation, God gives you a supernatural faith to believe the gospel. It is a gift from God, a gift of grace (Eph 2:8–9). And it is no temporary gift. He gives what is by nature a lasting faith—faith that endures to the end.

NATURAL FAITH VERSUS SUPERNATURAL FAITH

We live by natural faith every day. If you go to a restaurant, order something, and eat it, that is an act of faith. You don't know where it came from. You don't know what condition it's in. You don't know who cooked it. The same is true for your drink—they put something in a glass and tell you what it is, but you don't know that what they say is accurate. Still, you drink it. That's an act of faith.

If you get into an automobile and turn the ignition switch, you immediately set off a series of explosions—yet you have no fear that you might blow up, even though you have an internal combustion engine right at your knees. Instead, you go roaring onto the freeway at 65 miles an hour, full blast. Those are acts of faith.

If you go to the doctor and say, "Put me to sleep, cut me open, and take out anything you want," that's faith. You don't know the doctor or anybody else in the hospital, and you have no clue what they're doing in there. But you still put your faith in them. We live by faith all the time.

Those are all examples of an educated faith, a trained human faith. We've been around long enough to know that engines don't typically blow up and doctors don't usually take the wrong thing out.

But when it comes to putting your faith in Jesus Christ, you literally have to deny yourself and entrust your entire life in time and eternity to someone you've never seen. That requires a faith that is beyond normal human faith—it requires supernatural faith that is a gift from God. And the only kind of faith God gives is a faith that endures.

You could not muster up your own faith to be saved, nor could you muster up enough faith to *stay* saved. Were you to depend upon your own faith, it would fail you when God didn't do what you thought He ought to. Your own human faith would constantly become weaker and weaker—you would begin to question the truth when your experience didn't align with it.

It is the gift of faith from God that alone enables you to believe even when everything does not go as you think it should. Such enduring faith is inexplicable from a natural point of view. It has taken martyrs all the way to the stake. It has fortified Christians all the way to the guillotine.

Security in Christ, then, is tied to a faith that perseveres to the end. Any idea of salvation that leaves out security is a distortion of the truth. And any idea of security that leaves out perseverance is a distortion of the truth. You cannot have salvation without security, and you cannot have a secure salvation without unconquerable faith.

PETER'S TESTIMONY OF PERSEVERANCE

Before we look at any passage of Scripture in detail, I want to give you a bigger picture of the perseverance of the saints. And the life of Peter is a great place to start.

Any treatise on the perseverance of the saints should feature Peter because he was so prone to public failure—he frequently and obviously experienced the protection of a God-given, persevering faith.

From the gospels, it is evident that none of our Lord's disciples except Judas failed more miserably than Peter. Peter comes off as erratic, ambitious, selfish, vacillating, weak, cowardly, and hotheaded. On several occasions, he invited strong rebukes from the Lord.

None was more severe than when Jesus looked him in the face and said, "Get behind Me, Satan!" (Matt 16:23). When the Lord identifies you as a tool of Satan, you have seriously stumbled. Jesus said this to Peter right after the disciple made the greatest confession of his life: "You are the Christ, the Son of the living God" (v. 16). And Jesus had responded, "Flesh and blood did not reveal this to you, but My Father who is in heaven" (v. 17).

Another monumental failure in Peter's life was his repeated denial of Christ. Jesus had told Peter that he would deny Him three times (Matt 26:34), and before the night was over, despite his initial protestations, Peter emphatically did just that (vv. 35, 69–74). It wasn't long after those denials that he went out and wept bitterly, desperately wanting to be restored (v. 75).

After His resurrection, Jesus met with the apostles at the Sea of Galilee. John 21:2 says, "Simon Peter, and Thomas called Didymus, and Nathanael of Cana in Galilee, and the sons of Zebedee, and two others of His disciples were together." Verse 3 explains that Peter had gone back to fishing—back to his old career before he met Christ—and the other disciples joined him.

But they couldn't catch anything, even though they knew that lake very well. Then Jesus arrived and asked the question no unsuccessful fisherman ever wants to hear: "You do not have any fish, do you?" (v. 5). The disciples did not know their questioner was Jesus at this point, but He said to them in verse 6, "Cast the net on the right-hand side of the boat and you will find a catch." They did so and were immediately overloaded with fish, and Peter, realizing that it was Christ, jumped from the boat to swim to the shore (v. 7).

Peter was in a hurry to be restored. He hated the sin that he saw in himself so much that he impetuously dove in, even though they were a mere hundred yards from the shore (v. 8).

After the disciples were reunited with Christ and had eaten the breakfast He provided them, John records a conversation between our Lord and Peter. Verses 15–17 read,

> Jesus said to Simon Peter, "Simon, son of John, do you love Me more than these?" He said to Him, "Yes, Lord; You know that I love You." He said to him, "Tend My lambs." He said to him again a second time, "Simon, son of John, do you love Me?" He said to Him, "Yes, Lord; You know that I love You." He said to him, "Shepherd My sheep." He said to him the third time, "Simon, son of John, do you love Me?"

At this point, verse 17 says Peter was grieved because the Lord asked this question three times. But he finally responds, "Lord, You know all things; You know that I love You." And Jesus replies,

"Tend My sheep." God Himself had given Peter an enduring faith and an enduring love for Christ. Was Peter's faith weak and vacillating? Yes, but never completely and never finally. We see this even in his great eagerness, each time, to be restored.

Not only was Peter restored, but Jesus closes this interaction by speaking of Peter's future crucifixion, which would glorify God (vv. 18–19). Peter would be faithful to the end. When it came time for his execution, he wouldn't let them crucify him upright because he didn't think he was worthy to be crucified like his Lord. So they crucified him upside down, which was an even more excruciating way to die.

Peter is a great example of the highs and lows of the Christian life. He is proof that a true believer can stumble seriously. But because he was protected by an enduring faith produced in his heart by God's sovereign work, he never failed completely or finally.

THE REASON FOR PETER'S PERSEVERANCE

Jesus told Peter he was going to face difficulties. He told the disciple in Luke 22:31, "Simon, Simon, behold, Satan has demanded permission to sift you like wheat." Satan can't do anything to us without God's permission because he is God's servant. He can do nothing that God does not allow.

Satan wanted to tear into Peter. But verse 32 gives us Jesus' unforgettable answer. Satan demanded permission to sift Peter like wheat, and Jesus responds, "But I have prayed for you, that your faith may not fail." If that's what Jesus prays, that's what will happen—Peter's faith would never fail.

Satan could not have tempted Peter if the Lord had not allowed it. And the Lord did allow it, knowing Peter's faith could not fail because He prayed that it wouldn't. Jesus' prayers are always answered by the Father because Jesus always prays according to the Father's will, just as the Spirit intercedes according to the Father's will (see John 11:42).

So Jesus prayed for Peter's faith not to fail—but what about our faith? Does God preserve us as well? To answer that question, we can look to Christ's prayer in John 17.

Here you find the Lord praying His great high-priestly prayer. We see in verses 9–10, "I ask on their behalf; I do not ask on behalf of the world, but of those whom You have given Me; for they are Yours; and all things that are Mine are Yours, and Yours are Mine; and I have been glorified in them." Jesus is praying specifically for believers.

He continues in verse 11, "I am no longer in the world; and yet they themselves are in the world, and I come to You. Holy Father, keep them in Your name." What an amazing prayer! Jesus prays, "Father, keep *them*," not just Peter. If you are a true believer, you were included in that prayer. Jesus has already prayed that your faith would not fail.

He prays even more specifically down in verse 15, "I do not ask You to take them out of the world, but to keep them from the evil one." This is Jesus in action, interceding as the great High Priest on our behalf, asking the Father to protect us—that our faith fail not.

We know that Jesus prayed this prayer for *all* believers because He says so in verse 20: "I do not ask on behalf of these alone, but for those also who believe in Me through their word." We believe in Him through the words that were written by the apostles, so this prayer secures us.

It is not an oddity that the Lord Jesus Christ is interceding for Peter in Luke 22; it's the same intercession that He carries out in John 17, the same intercession He made for His apostles and still makes now for all whom the Father would bring to salvation through their preaching as well.

Furthermore, John 17 was no one-off prayer that Jesus offered. He prays like that today—and every day. Hebrews 7:25 says, "He is able also to save forever those who draw near to God through Him, since He always lives to make intercession for them." Jesus' prayer in John 17 is one He continues to pray at all times. He *is presently* our great High Priest, at the right hand of the Father, interceding for us. And He is able to save us forever. We are kept by an enduring faith that is sustained and maintained to the end by the intercession of the Lord Jesus Christ Himself, according to the will of His Father.

The Holy Spirit has a similar ministry. Romans 8:26–27 teaches that "in the same way the Spirit also helps our weakness; for we do not know how to pray as we should, but the Spirit Himself intercedes for us with groanings too deep for words; and He who searches the hearts knows what the mind of the Spirit is, because He intercedes for the saints according to the will of God." This is a silent, intra-Trinitarian communion wherein the Spirit intercedes on our behalf.

So Christ prays that our faith not fail, that the Father keep us. The Spirit intercedes for us as well. And as a result, verses 28–30 conclude,

> And we know that God causes all things to work together for good to those who love God, to those who are called according to His purpose. For those whom He foreknew, He also predestined to become conformed to the image of His Son, so that He would be the firstborn among many brethren; and these whom He predestined, He also called; and these whom He called, He also justified; and these whom He justified, He also glorified.

Christ's intercession guarantees our future glory. The Holy Spirit's intercession guarantees our future glory. And the Father's purpose guarantees our future glory. God didn't save you for a temporary enterprise; He saved you to conform you to the image of His Son in eternal glory.

We have been chosen, called, justified, sanctified, and we will be glorified. We are kept until that hour, and we are kept by an enduring faith sustained by the intercessory work of Jesus Christ. He prays that we will be protected from anything that would assault our faith, whether it be the flesh, the world, or Satan himself. Added to Christ's intercession is the intercession of the Holy Spirit, who is praying in ways that we can't. God hears and answers those prayers and causes everything to work out for good.

Persevering faith preserved Peter in his trial, and it's why there's no one better suited to write about it than the apostle. This was the man so pained by his own failure that he dove into the sea to swim to Jesus for restoration. It is only fitting for him to be the one to teach us about persevering faith.

PETER'S TEACHING ON PERSEVERANCE

Peter wrote his first epistle to believers who were facing imminent trials. In 1 Peter 2:20, he writes about being harshly treated and enduring it with patience. In 3:14, he writes about harm that could befall them. In 4:16, he writes about them suffering as Christians—not feeling ashamed, but glorifying God.

The letter recognizes that these believers were under grave intimidation and threat. And their concern was whether their faith would survive. They didn't trust in their own strength because they knew their own struggles as believers. They lived, as we all do, in Romans 7:14–24, battling the remaining flesh. They wondered whether they would be able to persist under extreme persecution. They feared their faith might fail.

Thus, Peter wrote to these suffering believers to teach them about the nature of their faith and the certainty of their salvation. Later we will look at a handful of biblical texts on perseverance, but 1 Peter 1:3–9 gives us an introduction to the doctrine. This rich text expands before our very eyes as we read it. It is something of a doxology, much like the end of Jude—a pronunciation of glorious blessing on God for our eternal salvation.

> Blessed be the God and Father of our Lord Jesus Christ, who according to His great mercy has caused us to be born again to a living hope through the resurrection of Jesus Christ from the dead, to obtain an inheritance which is imperishable and undefiled and will not fade away, reserved in heaven for you, who are protected by the power of God through faith for a salvation ready to be revealed in the last time. In this you greatly rejoice, even though now for a little while, if necessary, you have been distressed by various trials, so that the proof of your faith, being more precious than gold which is perishable, even though tested by fire, may be found to result in praise and glory and honor at the revelation of Jesus Christ; and though you have not seen Him, you love Him, and though you do not see Him now, but believe in Him, you greatly rejoice with joy inexpressible and full of glory, obtaining as the outcome of your faith the salvation of your souls.

"In this you greatly rejoice," verse 6 says—who wouldn't! We greatly rejoice that we are protected and will surely receive a glorious inheritance in Christ Jesus. In these few verses, Peter gives us six elements of our protection as believers.

First, Peter says we are protected through a living hope. "Blessed be the God and Father of our Lord Jesus Christ, who according to His great mercy has caused us to be born again to a living hope through the resurrection of Jesus Christ from the dead" (v. 3).

We have been born again. That means we have been given new, eternal life, which is not just a duration of life, but a kind of life. It is the life of God in us. Everything becomes supernaturally and spiritually alive: Our joy is a living joy, our peace is a living peace, and our hope is a living hope. Ours is the opposite of a hope that dies; we possess a hope that lives and *cannot* die.

In verse 13 of this same chapter, Peter says, "Prepare your minds for action, keep sober in spirit, fix your hope completely on the grace to be brought to you at the revelation of Jesus Christ." He's telling believers to stop worrying about the tribunal of men and to start fixing their hope on the grace that will be theirs at the revelation of Jesus Christ.

In verses 3–4, we have "a living hope [secured] through the resurrection of Jesus Christ from the dead, to obtain an inheritance which is imperishable and undefiled and will not fade away, reserved in heaven for you." Our eternal life has been secured by our Lord's conquering of death.

I love the fact that Peter doesn't limit himself to just one statement on the security of our inheritance. It would be enough to say, "You have a living hope through the resurrection of Jesus Christ from the dead to obtain an inheritance." But he adds, "which is imperishable," in case you were wondering. Then, if you're still wondering, he adds "undefiled" and "will not fade away," as well as "reserved in heaven for you."

We're guaranteed an "imperishable" inheritance, which simply means it's not liable to corruption. Neither can it be plundered by an enemy (see John 10:28–29; Rom 8:35–39). Our inheritance can't be stolen by adversaries. It is eternal because it is protected by God. Then Peter adds the word "undefiled," which means "unstained, not subject to defect." And finally, he says that our inheritance "will not fade away." In short, he says our salvation is protected in every way.

We find this same truth in Ephesians 1. Most Bible scholars say verses 3 through 14 form one sentence, which means Paul was writing with intensity. This great passage begins in verse 3, "Blessed be the God and Father of our Lord Jesus Christ, who has blessed us with every spiritual blessing in the heavenly places in Christ." What is included in "every spiritual blessing?" Verse 4 explains, "He chose us in Him before the foundation of the world, that we would be holy and blameless before Him." Before the world began, before time began, God chose us to be with Him in glory—so He will get us there.

Paul continues in verses 5–6, "He predestined us to adoption as sons through Jesus Christ to Himself, according to the kind intention of His will, to the praise of the glory of His grace." God determined in eternity past that He would bring us to glory. This is His will for all believers.

In verse 11, Paul says, like Peter, "We have obtained an inheritance." It's an inheritance that we were predestined to before time began. Our eternal destiny was locked up—sealed and delivered, as it were—before the world was created.

Paul explains that this inheritance was "according to His purpose who works all things after the counsel of His will, to the end that we who were the first to hope in Christ would be to the praise of His glory. In Him, you also, after listening to the message of truth, the gospel of your salvation—having also believed, you were sealed in Him with the Holy Spirit of promise" (vv. 11–13). When you call the Spirit "the Holy Spirit of promise," you are recognizing Him as a seal that guarantees the future—as yet unrealized. The Holy Spirit of promise was given as "a pledge," Paul adds in verse 14. That's the Greek word *arrabōn*, which refers to a down payment (see 2 Cor 1:22; 5:5).

You were given the Holy Spirit as a pledge—a guarantee—the moment you believed. Understand, then, that the moment you believed, you were sealed so that your inheritance will never change. That's the way God planned it in eternity past, that is His unchanging will, and that is exactly what He will accomplish.

Over in Ephesians 4:30, Paul adds, "Do not grieve the Holy Spirit of God, by whom you were sealed for the day of [final] redemption." You have been given a living hope, an inheritance that can never change, and you have been sealed forever by the Spirit.

You are protected by the power of God through a living hope.

Secondly, we are protected by God's own power. We see this in 1 Peter 1:5, where Peter says we are "protected by the power of God through faith for a salvation ready to be revealed in the last time." The key word here is "protected"; that's the heart of the passage. Peter is blessing God for divine protection.

"Protected" in this verse comes from the Greek word *phroureō*. This strong military term means "to guard," as of soldiers guarding prisoners (cf. 2 Cor 11:32; Gal 3:23). It's also a present-tense participle, which indicates that believers are constantly guarded. Those who belong to God are perpetually shielded from all enemies until the war is over and the victory is complete.

They are protected, verse 5 says, "by the power of God through faith for a salvation ready to be revealed at the last time." Notice how protection and faith are tied together: The protection comes to us through faith. In verse 5, you are "protected by the power of God *through faith*." In verse 8, no matter what is going on, you "*believe* in Him." In verse 9, the "outcome of *your faith*" is the salvation of your soul. By "salvation" here he means final salvation: glorification.[40]

Not only are believers protected by God through faith, they are also protected "for a salvation ready to be revealed in the last time"

(v. 5). We are protected by the power of God until our salvation is complete—God guards us until we see Christ in His glory.

Philippians 1:6 says, "He who began a good work in you will perfect it until the day of Christ Jesus." "The day of Christ Jesus" is the same as the day of final redemption—the day we see Christ and enter into eternal glory. It's the day that John had in mind in 1 John 3:2, "Beloved, now we are children of God, and it has not appeared as yet what we will be. We know that when He appears, we will be like Him, because we will see Him just as He is."

We find this in 2 Timothy 4:7–8, "I have fought the good fight, I have finished the course, I have kept the faith; in the future there is laid up for me the crown of righteousness, which the Lord, the righteous Judge, will award to me on that day; and not only to me, but also to all who have loved His appearing." We are sealed until final salvation—glorification—is ours. We are kept by divine power—the very power of God Himself—until Christ's appearing.

This draws our minds to one other passage: Romans 8, probably the greatest chapter on the perseverance of the saints. Consider Romans 8:38–39, "I am convinced that neither death, nor life, nor angels, nor principalities, nor things present, nor things to come, nor powers, nor height, nor depth, nor any other created thing, will be able to separate us from the love of God, which is in Christ Jesus our Lord." There is no power that can conquer the power of God and His love for His own.

Thirdly, we are protected by trials. This truth seems counterintuitive, but I want to show you how important it is. It encapsulates the heart and soul of perseverance.

First Peter 1:6 says, "In this you greatly rejoice." Of course, we rejoice that we're protected by God's power through a living hope. But Peter continues, "In this you greatly rejoice, even though now for a little while, if necessary, you have been distressed by various trials."

Trials differ from person to person because we all have different spiritual needs. We are at various points along the path of spiritual development, so the Lord commissions hardships according to what each individual needs for sanctification—and we rejoice in those trials. That's why Peter says we will experience trials "if necessary."

Peter tells these people that, instead of looking at the possibility of being arrested, tortured, and martyred, and fearing their faith would fail, they are to "*rejoice*." Then he gives the reason for rejoicing in verse 7: "So that the proof of your faith, being more precious than gold which is perishable, even though tested by fire, may be found to result in praise and glory and honor at the revelation of Jesus Christ."

The first part of that verse shows us that faith is proven through trials. Here's a way to understand it: God does not sustain our faith by keeping it away from trials, but rather the opposite. God sustains our faith by putting it through hard times. He sustains our faith *by means* of trials. When you come through a trial trusting the Lord, you gain confidence that your salvation is the real thing.

The phrase "you greatly rejoice" (v. 6) might catch you by surprise. We tend to get it backward, thinking that rejoicing is for when we *don't* go through trials. That is certainly the message of today's prosperity preachers, who give people the false hope of success, ease, and comfort instead of preparing them for suffering. But Peter's message opposes such false prophets.

Remember, Peter was writing to people facing life-threatening persecutions. Fear would have been the natural response. But Peter says, "You greatly rejoice." Why? Because these tests prove the character of your faith. Human, superficial faith will disintegrate, while God-given faith will endure.

We see this in the parable of the soils (Matt 13:1–23). Some of the seed went into shallow soil that sat on top of a rock bed (vv. 5, 20). It sprung up for a little while, but when persecution came, it withered and died (vv. 6, 21). Persecution and trials always test the authenticity of spiritual life.

James 1:2–3 says essentially the same thing. "Consider it all joy, my brethren, when you encounter various trials, knowing that the testing of your faith produces endurance." When I was very young, the devil would hammer me with doubts. But I don't question the character of my faith anymore because it has withstood so many trials. That is a marvelous advantage of testing: Every time you go through a trial, you see the nature of your faith.

Make no mistake, trials don't help *God* find out what kind of faith you have. He needs no information about your faith—He gave it to you! It's that trials become a joy to you because they produce endurance, and endurance has a perfecting result in you (vv. 3–4).

That is wonderful news. What is a greater gift than the assurance of salvation? If you have ever doubted that you are saved, you know how comforting it is to firmly know that your faith is genuine. Temporary suffering is a small price to pay for confidence that our salvation is secure. That is why it's so valuable to see our faith's capability to survive disaster. In fact, I have found in my own life that the more severe the trial, the stronger my faith is, and the more my confidence in God rises.

Romans 8:35–36 says, "Who will separate us from the love of Christ?" In other words, is there anything that can cause Christ to stop loving us? "Will tribulation, or distress, or persecution, or famine, or nakedness, or peril, or sword?" Those were all trials Paul endured in his life. He records them in 2 Corinthians 11:23–28.

> In far more labors, in far more imprisonments, beaten times without number, often in danger of death. Five times I received from the Jews thirty-nine lashes. Three times I was beaten with rods, once I was stoned, three times I was shipwrecked, a night and a day I have spent in the deep. I have been on frequent journeys, in dangers from rivers, dangers from robbers, dangers from my countrymen, dangers from the Gentiles, dangers in the city, dangers in the wilderness, dangers on the sea, dangers among false brethren; I have been in labor and

> hardship, through many sleepless nights, in hunger and thirst, often without food, in cold and exposure. Apart from such external things, there is the daily pressure on me of concern for all the churches.

And what does Paul say about living through such trials? Romans 8:37, "But in all these things we overwhelmingly conquer through Him who loved us." The faith that God gives us rises above trials.

Now trials do produce distress for a little while; we see that in 1 Peter 1:6. But verse 7 tells us they come like fire to burn off the dross. Not only do they reveal our faith, but they purify it. What emerges is a faith that is "more precious than gold which is perishable, even though tested by fire." So instead of asking God to remove you from trials, you should ask Him to put you through all the trials necessary to give you the confidence that your faith is real.

The fourth way God protects our faith is by eternal purpose. I've said something about this already, so I don't need to belabor the point.

The end of 1 Peter 1:7 teaches us that our faith will "be found to result in praise and glory and honor at the revelation of Jesus Christ." That is an amazing promise. Our faith is designed to survive to the end.

We have a proven, tested faith that will find its fulfillment at the revealing of the Lord Jesus Christ. That is the reason we were saved in the first place—we were chosen so that we would be brought to eternal glory (Rom 8:17, 30).

We will be made like Christ (1 John 3:2). We will be given a glorified body (1 Cor 15:42–43). We will go to the place He's preparing for us (John 14:2–3). That is what we eagerly await, not the things of this life; we're not citizens here (Phil 3:20). We cry out for the redemption of our body because we know what God has prepared for those that love Him (Rom 8:23). And God's pledge is to bring us to that eternal glory.

We must understand our salvation in three dimensions—past, present, and future. There is past salvation at the point when you first believe. There is present salvation in the process by which you are kept. And there is future and final salvation in which you are glorified. When God predetermined to save you, He predetermined that all three would take place, not merely some part of them. That's why Paul says in Romans 8:18, "I consider that the sufferings of this present time are not worthy to be compared with the glory that is to be revealed to us." Whatever we might suffer here, we rejoice because no amount of suffering compares to the glory that God predetermined for us. Nothing can take salvation away.

Fifth, we're protected by undying love. First Peter 1:8 says, "And though you have not seen Him, you love Him." This is a profound statement about the nature of true salvation. True salvation is characterized not only by faith in Christ, but by loving Him.

You can believe the facts of the gospel and not be saved—as the demons do (Mark 5:7; Jas 2:19). The issue is in loving the Lord Jesus Christ. Though you have not seen Him, you love Him.

To define Christianity in its purest sense, you'd have to use that word, *love*. You could talk about believing in Christ, but that's not enough because many people say they believe in Him. I once read an article in which a man claimed there are three billion Christians in the world. There are probably three billion people who believe in Jesus in some sense, but I'm quite sure there aren't that many who *love* Him.

The Christian's love for Christ overflows with joy. That's why Peter says in this verse, "You love Him, and though you do not see Him now, but believe in Him, you greatly rejoice with joy inexpressible and full of glory." Why do we sing? Because we're filled with joy. Whom do we sing about? Christ, the source of our joy.

I like praise choruses, but so many of them are drawn from the Old Testament. Of course, I don't mind singing about the Old Testament, but I prefer to get to the best part—Christ. He's the one we love.

When Jesus restored Peter at the Sea of Galilee, He asked him one question, "Do you love Me?" (John 21:17). Jesus saw love as the defining feature of their relationship. After Jesus asked the question three times, Peter said, "Lord, You know all things; You know that I love You." I like that response. Peter knew that Jesus is omniscient.

So he appealed to the fact that the Lord already knew what was in his heart. In the same way, Christ knows if we love Him.

First John 4:19 says, "We love, because He first loved us." There's no such thing as a Christian who doesn't love Christ, because love is the response of those who have *been loved* by Him. And we continue to grow in our love for Him.

In Romans 8, again, Paul knew nothing could separate him from Christ's love for him, but he also knew that nothing could separate him from his love for Christ. Believers can be struck with tribulation, distress, persecution, nakedness, famine, and sword, and their love for Christ will not be damaged—because we love Him with a love that He gave us (Rom 5:5). It's a gift from God, just like faith. You've been given a love from God that remains strong—it is an undying love.

Finally, 1 Peter 1:9 reveals the sixth way our salvation is protected. Peter writes in verses 8–9, "You love Him, and though you do not see Him now, but believe in Him, you greatly rejoice with joy inexpressible and full of glory, obtaining as the outcome of your faith the salvation of your souls."

Peter says that final salvation is "the outcome of *your faith.*" That's why we say this doctrine should be called *the perseverance of the saints* or *the perseverance of faith.*

You have been given a faith that never perishes, that is protected by the power of God. It can't be overthrown because it is strengthened through trials. And it is designed to result in eternal glory which was promised before the world began. It is a faith accompanied by an undying love for Christ, and it will obtain the final salvation of our souls.

There is simply no escape from this reality: The result of saving faith is final salvation. Just as your salvation in the past and present was and is a result of faith, so final salvation will be yours, because this faith will endure to the very end. That is the nature of supernatural saving faith. It is nothing less than a permanent gift from God.

THE BIBLICAL SUPPORT FOR PERSEVERANCE

Many biblical passages beyond the writings of Peter support this glorious truth. For instance, Matthew 18:12–14 says,

> What do you think? If any man has a hundred sheep, and one of them has gone astray, does he not leave the ninety-nine on the mountains and go and search for the one that is straying? If it turns out that he finds it, truly I say to you, he rejoices over it more than over the ninety-nine which have not gone astray. So it is not the will of your Father who is in heaven that one of these little ones perish.

"Little ones" in this chapter means believers—in verse 6, Jesus refers to "these little ones who believe in Me." That's who

Jesus has in mind when He says in verse 14, "It is not the will of your Father who is in heaven that one of these little ones perish."

Our Lord affirms that same promise in John 10:27. Jesus says, "My sheep hear my voice, and I *know* them" (emphasis added). By saying "know," Jesus meant more than, "I know who they are." That statement would be true of everyone, but He is talking about a specific group here. The rest of Scripture bears out that to "know" them means to "have an intimate and personal union and relationship with" them. Jesus continues through verses 27–28, "I know them, and they follow Me; and I give eternal life to them, and they will never perish."

In Matthew 18, Jesus said it is not the will of His Father that any believer should perish, and in John 10, He likewise says they shall never perish. But He strengthens this statement in verses 28–30, "And no one will snatch them out of My hand. My Father, who has given them to Me, is greater than all; and no one is able to snatch them out of the Father's hand. I and the Father are one." We are securely held in the secure hands of the Father and the Son.

John 4:14, says, "Whoever drinks of the water that I will give him shall never thirst; but the water that I will give him will become in him a well of water springing up to eternal life." Once the well is opened up, it never runs dry—that's why the believer will "never thirst." It is a wellspring of eternal life.

In the next chapter of John, Jesus says, "Truly, truly, I say to you, he who hears My word, and believes Him who sent Me, has eternal life, and does not come into judgment, but has passed out of death into life" (John 5:24). Jesus explains the same idea in John 3:16 and 18, "For God so loved the world, that He gave His only begotten Son, that whoever believes in Him shall not perish, but have eternal life.... He who believes in Him is not judged." There is no judgment—no condemnation—for those who believe.

Another text which expresses this reality is John 6:37–40,

> All that the Father gives Me will come to Me, and the one who comes to Me I will certainly not cast out. For I have come down from heaven, not to do My own will, but the will of Him who sent Me. This is the will of Him who sent Me, that of all that He has given Me I lose nothing, but raise it up on the last day. For this is the will of My Father, that everyone who beholds the Son and believes in Him will have eternal life, and I Myself will raise him up on the last day.

No one falls through the cracks in the process of salvation. Whom the Father chooses, He draws. Whom He draws, He draws to Christ. Whoever is drawn to Christ comes, and, when he comes, Christ receives him, keeps him, and raises him on the last day. No believer is lost along the way. The reality of this doctrine drove Charles Spurgeon to great joy:

> When I heard it said that the Lord would keep His people right to the end,—that Christ had said, "My sheep hear My voice, and I know them, and they follow Me: and I give unto them eternal life; and they shall never perish, neither shall any

> pluck them out of My hand," I must confess that the doctrine of the final preservation of the saints was a bait that my soul could not resist. I thought it was a sort of life insurance—an insurance of my character, an insurance of my soul, an insurance of my eternal destiny. I knew that I could not keep myself, but if Christ promised to keep me, then I should be safe for ever; and I longed and prayed to find Christ, because I knew that, if I found Him, He would not give me a temporary and trumpery salvation, such as some preach, but eternal life which could never be lost, the living and incorruptible seed which liveth and abideth for ever, for no one and nothing "shall be able to separate us from the love of God, which is in Christ Jesus our Lord."[41]

In John 17:11, Jesus says, "I am no longer in the world; and yet they themselves"—those who belong to Him—"are in the world, and I come to You. Holy Father, keep them in Your name, the name which You have given Me, that they may be one even as We are."

Jesus was headed to the cross, and His prayer was that the Father would keep them and bring them into glory. In verse 15 He says, "I do not ask You to take them out of the world, but to keep them from the evil one." He was asking the Father to seal their faith and their salvation.

In 1 Corinthians 1:8 we read that those who are in Christ are confirmed "to the end, blameless in the day of our Lord Jesus Christ." We do sin, but our sins have been covered by Christ, and we are left blameless (v. 30).

Paul adds in verse 9, "God is faithful, through whom you were called into fellowship with His Son, Jesus Christ our Lord." This is the key: *God is faithful*. He called you in order to confirm you all the way to the end and bring you blameless into His eternal presence. *His* faithfulness guarantees your salvation.

In Colossians 1:5, Paul says believers have a "hope laid up for you in heaven." Your hope is in heaven, held for you there until you are glorified.

First Thessalonians 5:23 says, "Now may the God of peace Himself sanctify you entirely; and may your spirit and soul and body be preserved complete, without blame at the coming of our Lord Jesus Christ." Again, this truth is on display—the God who sanctified us will preserve us complete and blameless for when our Lord Jesus Christ reappears. The next verse also emphasizes this thought: "Faithful is He who calls you, and He also will bring it to pass" (v. 24). He was faithful to call you into salvation; He will be faithful to preserve you until that salvation is complete.

True believers remain not because they have the power on their own to do it—they don't—but because the same God who called and justified them has promised to glorify them. If someone professes faith in Christ but falls away, it is not due to a failure on God's part; it is an indication that they were never saved to begin with. Remember 1 John 2:19, "They went out from us, but they were not really of us; for if they had been of us, they would have remained with us; but they went out, so that it would be shown that they all are not of us."

Paul closes 2 Thessalonians 2:16–17 with these words, "Now may our Lord Jesus Christ Himself and God our Father, who has loved us and given us eternal comfort and good hope by grace, comfort and strengthen your hearts." You're not supposed to live in fear that you'll somehow lose your salvation through the devil's work or your own weakness. That's not God's intention for you. He loves you, and He's given you eternal hope which should comfort and strengthen your heart.

Paul opens his epistle to Titus with another attestation to this doctrine. "Paul, a bond-servant of God and an apostle of Jesus Christ, for the faith of those chosen of God and the knowledge of the truth which is according to godliness, in the hope of eternal life, which God, who cannot lie, promised long ages ago" (Titus 1:1–2). Before you ever lived, even before creation, God promised eternal life—and He cannot lie. If any true believers are lost at any point, then God's promise in eternity past was deceitful. But that is impossible—the hope He gives us in salvation will never fail (Heb 6:19).

OBJECTIONS TO PERSEVERANCE

The bottom line of this doctrine is that salvation is forever. By its very nature, it is irrevocable.

In spite of the clarity of Scripture, however, many in the church today have fallen under the influence of teaching that denies this doctrine. As a result, they live in fear of losing their salvation. They are warned that they can, by sin or wavering faith, forfeit that salvation which God has given them. They are taught that a believer can become an unbeliever, a new creation in Christ can revert to the old, the children of God can become the children of the devil again, and citizens of heaven can become occupants of hell. In fact, according to this teaching, *everything* that is given to us in Christ can be lost.

Inevitably, those who teach such things endeavor to support them with Scripture, appealing to several passages to argue their point. I've had to deal with those supposedly biblical arguments throughout the years. On one occasion, I was in Minsk, Belarus, to speak at a pastors' conference being held at an old military camp—where Communist soldiers were once trained, pastors were now being trained. I was there for a week, sleeping in the barracks and teaching the Word of God.

Along the way, I made a side comment about the fact that salvation was eternal and could not be lost. At the end of the day, after a little bit of refreshment, I returned to my room and slept.

When I got up the next morning, the person directing the conference told me that I caused no small stir by saying that salvation is irrevocable—twenty-seven of the leaders stayed up all night discussing what I had said. Overnight, they had compiled a list of Scripture verses that made it difficult for them to accept this doctrine. And they wanted me to deal with each of the passages they had compiled.

That was a fair request. If this doctrine were true, it could stand the test of Scripture, and they were right to expect me to show them. So I tried my best to work through those verses, explaining why none of them taught that salvation can be lost.

Especially if you have been convinced that you can lose your salvation, you probably know some of those verses. It's important for us to look at them now and understand them in context.

TROUBLING VERSES[42]

Let's start with John 8:31. In this verse, Jesus says, "If you continue in My word, then you are truly disciples of Mine." Some interpret this to mean that a true disciple of Jesus *ceases* to be a disciple if he does not continue in Jesus' word. In a similar vein, John 15:6 says, "If anyone does not abide [i.e., remain] in Me, he is thrown away as a branch and dries up; and they gather them, and cast them into the fire and they are burned." According to some, this refers to a true believer who ends up going to hell because he is unfaithful.

Then there's Matthew 24:13: "The one who endures to the end, he will be saved." So, they'll say, your salvation depends entirely upon your endurance—it will last only as long as your endurance does (cf. 10:22). A similar statement appears in Acts 13:43, where Paul and Barnabas were speaking to Jews and God-fearing Gentiles, "urging them to continue in the grace of God." That could seem to imply that, in the end, salvation depends on *your* strength of will and commitment to Christ.

Romans 2:6–7 is another passage used to defend the idea of a salvation that can fail. It says God "will render to each person according to his deeds: to those who by perseverance in doing good seek for glory and honor and immortality, eternal life." Some people take those verses to mean that if you don't persevere in doing good, you will lose the eternal life God granted you.

Romans 11:22 says, "Behold then the kindness and severity of God; to those who fell, severity, but to you, God's kindness, if you continue in His kindness; otherwise you also will be cut off." Like the other passages, this one warns us to abide, remain, endure, and continue.

Paul adds in Colossians 1:21–23, "Although you were formerly alienated and hostile in mind, engaged in evil deeds, yet He has now reconciled you in His fleshly body through death, in order to present you before Him holy and blameless and beyond reproach—if indeed you continue in the faith firmly established and steadfast, and not moved away from the hope of the gospel that you have heard." Again, the word "continue" appears.

Hebrews 3:6 and 14 also comment on this issue. "Christ was faithful as a Son over His house—whose house we are, if we hold fast our confidence and ... our hope firm to the end.... For we have become partakers of Christ, if we hold fast the beginning of our assurance firm until the end."

All of these passages must be explained in relation to the doctrine of the perseverance of the saints. Are they warnings that if you drift, deviate, or fail to endure, you will lose your salvation? If so, then the Bible contradicts itself. Because as we've seen, Scripture teaches that saving faith perseveres and salvation is forever. Furthermore, it teaches that salvation is a work of God, not man—you can't save yourself, either in initiating your salvation or preserving it. And God's works never fail.

The point of these passages is not to warn believers that if they don't hang on with all their might they will lose their salvation. Rather, the point is that *those who persevere and hold fast to Christ give evidence that they are saved.* That understanding explains each passage.

Scripture clearly teaches that if you abide in Christ, then you are a real disciple. If you do not abide, you are not a true disciple. If you're one who endures, you're truly saved and will receive final salvation in the end. If you're one who continues in the grace of God and in the hope of the gospel, you give evidence of God's mighty saving work in you.

These passages define the nature of saving faith. They are not exhortations for true believers to secure their own salvation by "holding on." They are warnings to superficial believers, whose false faith will inevitably fail. But if your faith is real, it will endure to the end because it is given by God.

The same is true for Hebrews 6:4–10 and 10:26–31, which are commonly raised as objections to the doctrine of perseverance. These two controversial texts speak of those who identify as believers and experience certain blessings through their association with God's people, yet are not genuinely converted themselves. Thus, they apostatize from their false profession. But genuine believers persevere. Hence the author of Hebrews says that he was "convinced of better things concerning" the true believers among them (6:9).[43]

As we saw in 1 Peter 1:3–9, God protects us through faith. He gives us a faith that saves and that endures to the end. We were saved by faith, and we endure by faith, which is a gift of God (Eph 2:8–9).

The verses we just considered teach that the gift of supernatural faith perseveres. A text we've seen which confirms that interpretation is 1 John 2:19, "They went out from us, but they were not really of us, for if they had been of us, they would have remained with us; but they went out, so that it would be shown that they all are not of us." When somebody abandons the faith, it is proof that they *never possessed* real saving faith. It wasn't the faith that God gives because it didn't remain, abide, continue, hold fast, or endure.

Second Timothy 2:12 sheds light on this as well. "If we endure, we will also reign with Him; if we deny Him, He also will deny us." There are only two possibilities for people who profess Christ: They are genuine, or they are counterfeit. If we endure, we are genuine believers, and we'll reign. If we deny Him, we demonstrate our faith is a fake, and He will deny us. Remember what Jesus said: "Therefore everyone who confesses Me before men, I will also confess him before My Father who is in heaven. But whoever denies Me before men, I will also deny him before My Father who is in heaven" (Matt 10:32–33). Anyone who turns away from Christ after embracing Him for a time reveals that he never had real faith.

Those who do not endure are false professing believers—not true believers who have lost their salvation. The true believers are those who endure.

Of course, this does not mean that true believers will be free from temporary struggles with their faith. There are times when our faith is weak. But true faith will never fail completely or finally. As we saw earlier, Peter is a fitting example of this. Peter had real saving faith, but at times he also manifested weakness and even a temporary denial. If our faith is genuine, it may still be weak and temporarily falter, but as Paul writes in 2 Timothy 2:13, "If we are faithless, He remains faithful, for He cannot deny Himself."

NOW TO HIM WHO IS ABLE

To entertain the possibility that you could lose your salvation is to entertain a misrepresentation of God's grace. It's a misrepresentation of the nature of faith, the gift of God's love, and the work of Christ and the Spirit. The guarantee of Scripture, and therefore the promise of God, is that salvation is forever.

Nor is this a standalone doctrine—it has major implications for other primary doctrines. To get the perseverance of the saints wrong is to disrupt the doctrines of election, justification, sanctification, and glorification. It is to unravel all the strands in the cord of salvation. That's why I said at the outset that the most important element in the whole range of salvation doctrines is this issue of the perseverance of the saints. It is, in the end, what makes salvation *salvation*, because it ensures we are saved forever.

Philippians 1:6, as we saw earlier, could not be clearer. "I am confident of this very thing, that He who began a good work in you will perfect it until the day of Christ Jesus." If God started it, He will finish it. That should be a tremendous source of comfort for all believers.

The debate surrounding this doctrine may make it seem as if Scripture is unclear about it, or that your belief on the issue is merely a matter of personal preference. But the fact is that this doctrine is a critical component in our understanding of salvation.

All the passages we looked at, and many more, should give us confidence that those who are genuinely the children of God through faith in Christ are secure in that relationship forever. If you believe in the Lord Jesus Christ, you will never perish. Salvation is the gift of eternal life, and those who receive it will never lose it.

It stuns me that this fact would ever be open to question. Yet many Christians have denied the sweetness of settled confidence by questioning—and rejecting—this doctrine. They have denied the joy of the confidence that they are saved forever.

So many have been told that they will be lost unless *they* hold on to their confession, unless *they* hold on to their faith, unless *they* keep on believing in their own strength. But that is impossible. The reality is, if I *could* lose my salvation, I *would*. I can't produce my salvation by an act of my own faith, and I can't sustain it, either.

It's a terrible thing to teach people that they will lose their salvation if they sin or don't hang on to it. How tightly do you have to hold on? What if you sin? You have to live righteously—but how righteously do you have to live? We all sin, so people get caught in unnecessary anxiety, wondering how far they can go in sin before they lose their salvation.

We are secure in our salvation by God's gift of a faith that perseveres. He doesn't give us the faith to save us and then remove it. He gives us faith as a permanent gift that endures, even in trials. That's why instead of only talking about eternal security, which is a true side of the doctrine in its own right, I would rather feature the side of the perseverance of the saints. God secures us eternally by giving us a faith that never fails.

We have our moments of doubt. We have our struggles. But never does our faith turn to complete doubt and final denial. We are secured by the same supernatural faith that was given to us to cause us to believe savingly, and we are sustained by that same gift of faith.

In Jeremiah 32:40, the Lord describes the New Covenant that He would make with His people. "I will make an everlasting covenant with them that I will not turn away from them, to do them good;

and I will put the fear of Me in their hearts so that they will not turn away from Me." God puts in our hearts a fear of Him *so that we will never turn away from Him*. That's why He calls the New Covenant an "everlasting covenant"—the salvation it provides will never end.

This rich truth should fill our hearts with joy. It certainly did for Jude, who closed his letter with a wonderful doxology testifying to the preserving grace of God. His words provide a fitting conclusion for our study of our Savior's enduring faithfulness:

> Now to Him who is able to keep you from stumbling, and to make you stand in the presence of His glory blameless with great joy, to the only God our Savior, through Jesus Christ our Lord, be glory, majesty, dominion and authority, before all time and now and forever. Amen. (Jude 24–25)

ENDNOTES

[1] John Calvin, *Commentaries on the Epistle of Paul the Apostle to the Romans*, trans. John Owen, vol. 19 of Calvin's Commentaries (Edinburgh: Calvin Translation Society, 1849), 261.

[2] https://thestateoftheology.com

[3] For more on this topic, including comments on the difficult interpretive issues in Romans 5:12–21, see John MacArthur, ed., *Essential Christian Doctrine: A Handbook on Biblical Truth* (Wheaton: Crossway, 2021), 251–56.

[4] Charles Spurgeon, "Human Inability," *New Park Street Pulpit*, 4 vols. (London: Alabaster and Passmore, 1859), 4:138.

[5] John Calvin, *Institutes of the Christian Religion*, Library of Christian Classics 20–21, ed. John T. McNeill, trans. Ford Lewis Battles, (Philadelphia: Westminster John Knox, 1960), 1.4.4.

[6] Martin Luther, *On the Bondage of the Will*, trans. Henry Cole (London: T. Bensly, 1823), 293, 295.

[7] D. Martyn Lloyd-Jones, *The Plight of Man and the Power of God* (Grand Rapids: Eerdmans, 1945), 87.

[8] Canons of Dort (1619), Head I and II (esp. rejection 4); Heidelberg Catechism (1563), Q8; Second Helvetic Confession (1566), 8.2; The Thirty-Nine Articles (1571), article 10.

[9] Martin Luther, *Luther's Works*, ed. Philip S. Watson, vol. 33 (Philadelphia: Fortress Press, 1972), 62.

[10] J. Stephen Yuille, ed., *The Works of William Perkins*, vol. 4 (Grand Rapids: Reformation Heritage Books, 2016), 391.

[11] John MacArthur and Richard Mayhue, eds., *Biblical Doctrine: A Systematic Summary of Bible Truth* (Wheaton: Crossway, 2017), 504–506. See pages 506 and following for more details on this topic.

[12] David Clotfelter, *Sinners in the Hands of a Good God: Reconciling Divine Judgment and Mercy* (Chicago: Moody, 2004), 124.

[13] For a more detailed explanation of God's perfect omniscience, see MacArthur and Mayhue, *Biblical Doctrine*, 174–77.

[14] Charles H. Spurgeon, "Election," *Sermons of the Rev. C. H. Spurgeon*, series 2, vol. 15 (New York: Sheldon, Blakeman, & Co., 1857), 84.

[15] Spurgeon, "Election," 84.

[16] Spurgeon, "Election," 85.

[17] Charles H. Spurgeon, "The Death of Christ," The New Park Street Pulpit, vol. 4 (London: Alabaster and Passmore, 1859), 70.

[18] John Owen, *The Death of Death in the Death of Christ* (Edinburgh: Banner of Truth Trust, 1959).

[19] J. I. Packer, "Saved by His Precious Blood: An Introduction to John Owen's *The Death of Death in the Death of Christ*," in J. I. Packer and Mark Dever, *In My Place Condemned He Stood: Celebrating the Glory of the Atonement* (Wheaton: Crossway, 2007), 123.

[20] Charles H. Spurgeon, "Particular Redemption," *The New Park Street Pulpit*, vol. 4 (London: Alabaster and Passmore, 1859), 135.

[21] John MacArthur, *The MacArthur New Testament Commentary: 1–3 John* (Chicago: Moody, 2007), 48–49).

[22] For more on this important passage, see John MacArthur and Richard Mayhue, *Biblical Doctrine: A Systematic Summary of Biblical Truth* (Wheaton: Crossway, 2017), 464–66.

[23] For more on the correct understanding of *world* and *all* in reference to the atonement, see MacArthur and Mayhue, *Biblical Doctrine*, 554–65.

[24] John MacArthur, *The MacArthur New Testament Commentary: 2 Peter and Jude* (Chicago: Moody, 2005), 73–74.

[25] Thomas Watson, *A Body of Divinity* (Edinburgh: Banner of Truth, 1958), 223.

[26] Westminster Confession of Faith, 10.1.

[27] John Murray, *Redemption Accomplished and Applied* (1955; repr., Grand Rapids: Eerdmans, 2015), 91.

[28] Norman L. Geisler, *Chosen But Free*, 2nd ed. (Bloomington, MN: Bethany, 2001).

[29] Jonathan Edwards, *Freedom of the Will* (London: Hamilton, Adams & Co., 1860), 80.

[30] The ESV, LSB, and CSB all correctly translate the perfect tense verb in this verse.

[31] https://www.alliancenet.org/cambridge-declaration

[32] James Montgomery Boice, *Whatever Happened to the Gospel of Grace?* (Wheaton: Crossway, 2001), 126–27.

[33] Michael D. McMullen, ed., *William Wilberforce: His Unpublished Spiritual Journals* (Ross-Shire, Great Britain: Christian Heritage, 2021), 331.

[34] John Owen, *The Works of John Owen*, ed. William H. Goold, vol. 9 (Edinburgh: Banner of Truth, 1965), 29.

[35] Westminster Confession of Faith, 17.

[36] Westminster Confession of Faith, 17.1.

[37] Westminster Confession of Faith, 17.1.

[38] Westminster Confession of Faith, 17.3.

[39] Unfortunately, this view is taught by many people who deny what has come to be called *lordship salvation*. For my treatment of this subject, see *The Gospel According to Jesus*, rev. ed. (Grand Rapids: Zondervan, 2008), and its follow-up volume

The Gospel According to the Apostles, 2nd ed. (Nashville: Thomas Nelson, 2000).

[40] For more on the doctrine of glorification, see John MacArthur and Richard Mayhue, *Biblical Doctrine: A Systematic Summary of Biblical Truth* (Wheaton: Crossway, 2017), 653–59.

[41] C. H. Spurgeon, "Danger, Safety, Gratitude," sermon no. 3,074, preached January 8, 1874, *The Metropolitan Tabernacle Pulpit* (repr., Pasadena, TX: Pilgrim Publications, 1978), 54:24.

[42] I offer longer explanations of Galatians 5, Hebrews 6, John 15, and Matthew 12 in my book *Saved Without a Doubt: Being Sure of Your Salvation* (Colorado Springs: David C. Cook, 2011), 27–45.

[43] For a more detailed explanation of these passages, see John MacArthur and Richard Mayhue, *Biblical Doctrine: A Systematic Summary of Biblical Truth* (Wheaton: Crossway, 2017), 648–49.

INDEXES

INDEX OF SCRIPTURE

INDEX OF SUBJECTS

JOHN MACARTHUR

is pastor-teacher of Grace Community Church in Los Angeles, California, Chancellor of The Master's University and Seminary, teacher and voice heard globally through his media ministry Grace to You, and author of numerous best-selling books, including his commentary series and The MacArthur Study Bible. He has spent over 50 years preaching through every verse of the New Testament and much of the Old Testament while being a featured speaker at conferences around the world. John and his wife Patricia have been married for over sixty years and have four children, fifteen grandchildren, and nine great-grandchildren.

JOHN MACARTHUR PUBLISHING GROUP
LOS ANGELES, CALIFORNIA